open**doors**

REPORT ON INTERNATIONAL EDUCATIONAL EXCHANGE

Hey-Kyung Koh Chin
Institute of International Education

OPEN DOORS is the only comprehensive information resource on over 582,000 international students in the United States in 2001/2002 and on the more than 154,000 U.S. students who studied abroad in 2000/2001. The Institute of International Education, the largest and most experienced U.S. higher education exchange agency, has conducted an annual statistical survey of the internationally mobile student population in the United States since 1948, with U.S. government support since 1972.

582,996 international students were in the U.S. in 2001/2002, a 6.4% increase over last year.

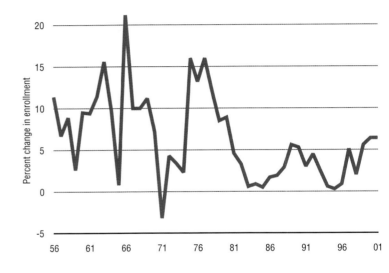

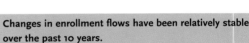

Changes in enrollment flows have been relatively stable over the past 10 years.

Academic Level	Int'l Students	Total U.S. Students*	% of U.S. Enrollment
Associate	67,667	4,754,674	1.4
Bachelor's	193,412	6,826,456	2.8
Graduate**	264,749	1,930,019	13.7

International students are 13.7% of all graduate enrollments in the U.S.

* College Board Annual Survey of Colleges for Fall 2001 enrollment

** Includes first professional degree

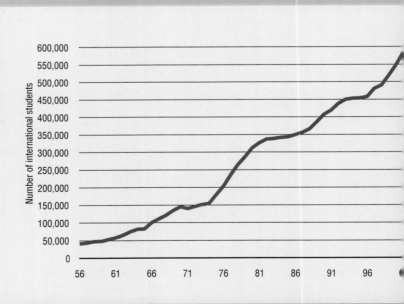

Since the 1950s, periods of steep growth have been followed by relatively long periods of minimal growth, with significant growth since 1998.

Year	Int'l Students	Annual % Change	Total Enrollment	% Int'l
1954/55	34,232	–	2,499,800	1.4
1959/60	48,486	2.6	3,402,300	1.4
1964/65	82,045	9.7	5,320,000	1.5
1969/70	134,959	11.2	7,978,400	1.7
1974/75	154,580	2.3	10,321,500	1.5
1979/80	286,343	8.5	11,707,000	2.4
1984/85	342,113	0.9	12,467,700	2.7
1985/86	343,777	0.5	12,387,700	2.8
1986/87	349,609	1.7	12,410,500	2.8
1987/88	356,187	1.9	12,808,487	2.8
1988/89	366,354	2.9	13,322,576	2.7
1989/90	386,851	5.6	13,824,592	2.8
1990/91	407,529	5.3	13,975,408	2.9
1991/92	419,585	3.0	14,360,965	2.9
1992/93	438,618	4.5	14,422,975	3.0
1993/94	449,749	2.5	14,473,106	3.1
1994/95	452,653	0.6	14,554,016	3.1
1995/96	453,787	0.3	14,419,252	3.1
1996/97	457,984	0.9	14,286,478	3.1
1997/98	481,280	5.1	13,294,221	3.6
1998/99	490,933	2.0	13,391,401	3.6
1999/00	514,723	4.8	13,584,998	3.8
2000/01	547,867	6.4	14,046,659	3.9
2001/02	582,996	6.4	13,511,149 **	4.3

The number of international students has risen sharply since 1954, but was just over 4% of total U.S. higher education enrollment in 2001/2002.

* In 1997 the College Board changed its data collection process.
** College Board Annual Survey of Colleges for Fall 2001 enrollment

THE BIG PICTURE

In general, the number of international students in the U.S. has increased each year, with plateaus in the mid-1980s and mid-1990s. This year's 6.4% growth in international enrollments builds on the same percentage increase from the previous year, 2000/01. The 12.8% increase seen over the past two years is the largest two-year rise since 1981.

While international student numbers have grown sharply since the early years of the census, their percentage of the total U.S. higher education enrollment has not grown proportionally. In 1954/55, international students made up 1.4% of U.S. higher education enrollment. Almost half a century and 17 times the number of students later, the percentage was just 4.3% in 2001/02. More than half of all international students are undergraduate students. International students comprise a larger proportion of the higher education enrollment total at the graduate levels (13.7%), and especially in certain disciplines.

For the purpose of the *Open Doors* International Student Census, international students are defined as those individuals who were enrolled for coursework at a U.S. institution of higher education under a temporary visa. These individuals may include spouses and dependents who arrive in the United States with the student if they take coursework, as well. They do not include refugees, immigrants, and permanent residents.

International education
$12 billion dollars to

State	Students 2001/2002	Tuition & Fees[1] 2001/2002	Living Exp. & Dependents[2] 2001/2002	Less U.S. Support[3] 2001/2002	Total Contribution 2001/2002	State	Students 2001/2002	Tuition & Fees[1] 2001/2002	Living Exp. & Dependents[2] 2001/2002	Less U.S. Support[3] 2001/2002	Contribu 2001/2
Alabama	6,040	46,544,146	85,238,123	34,494,543	97,287,725	Montana	944	8,781,002	14,076,403	4,992,943	17,864
Alaska	479	3,568,479	6,923,251	1,389,906	9,101,824	Nebraska	3,874	29,888,749	59,013,305	21,388,569	67,513
Arizona	10,507	89,125,406	180,178,816	84,739,199	184,565,024	Nevada	2,927	20,584,209	44,364,903	10,762,406	54,186
Arkansas	2,758	23,423,175	41,595,128	16,001,104	49,017,199	New Hampshire	2,436	39,602,987	41,468,821	20,508,841	60,562
California	78,741	827,054,078	1,331,138,869	528,546,027	1,629,646,919	New Jersey	13,516	152,936,621	244,295,501	107,882,028	289,350
Colorado	6,692	85,948,469	116,603,251	58,393,039	144,158,680	New Mexico	1,893	17,485,958	32,275,610	18,431,982	31,329
Connecticut	8,050	113,857,721	156,127,039	63,558,759	206,426,000	New York	62,053	850,625,653	1,132,017,723	619,296,369	1,363,347
Delaware	1,975	21,116,582	27,900,842	14,174,546	34,842,879	North Carolina	8,960	109,462,701	148,265,751	86,480,934	171,247
Dist. of Col.	9,241	142,351,670	182,677,599	93,165,129	231,864,140	North Dakota	1,357	9,383,483	18,769,687	6,715,343	21,437
Florida	28,303	288,047,769	453,998,159	177,178,738	564,867,190	Ohio	19,384	243,933,610	334,410,241	198,773,339	379,570
Georgia	11,991	140,786,301	195,430,762	102,791,805	233,425,258	Oklahoma	8,818	64,083,412	145,659,662	48,780,607	160,962
Guam	162	550,350	2,225,709	250,983	2,525,075	Oregon	6,560	74,430,024	101,908,397	46,492,767	129,845
Hawaii	5,289	42,773,202	93,946,122	30,808,787	105,910,537	Pennsylvania	24,014	389,135,369	411,737,276	253,435,487	547,437
Idaho	1,578	12,230,656	25,668,025	9,646,583	28,252,098	Puerto Rico	743	2,740,666	11,018,094	3,202,346	10,556
Illinois	25,498	339,534,541	475,156,422	286,591,932	528,099,031	Rhode Island	3,370	50,842,442	64,242,203	30,378,552	84,706
Indiana	12,871	167,744,301	234,895,462	131,755,836	270,883,927	South Carolina	3,731	35,825,415	64,869,996	33,380,375	67,315
Iowa	7,896	84,501,341	130,037,765	65,838,251	148,700,855	South Dakota	770	5,631,963	9,675,274	4,030,996	11,276
Kansas	7,244	53,850,850	125,223,967	49,019,855	130,054,963	Tennessee	5,867	69,991,040	91,818,618	40,952,319	120,857
Kentucky	4,789	39,730,758	63,979,396	28,048,453	75,661,701	Texas	44,192	315,454,378	681,478,120	258,906,505	738,025
Louisiana	6,312	65,460,046	94,279,909	49,191,182	110,548,773	Utah	5,950	32,688,394	96,524,122	33,217,916	95,994
Maine	1,357	14,191,132	22,500,276	9,904,896	26,786,512	Vermont	908	13,828,454	15,575,167	7,652,638	21,750
Maryland	13,947	150,280,761	228,160,798	83,287,808	295,153,750	Virgin Islands	105	859,950	1,902,623	321,521	2,441
Massachusetts	29,988	562,799,150	610,370,835	372,059,442	801,110,543	Virginia	12,600	136,345,360	204,345,933	79,507,383	261,183
Michigan	23,103	276,590,319	363,870,469	191,350,235	449,110,553	Washington	11,624	116,205,756	178,202,878	55,286,199	239,122
Minnesota	8,670	94,726,930	135,153,851	67,600,761	162,280,021	West Virginia	2,108	17,724,378	34,678,640	17,993,144	34,409
Mississippi	2,381	18,109,112	38,198,694	11,643,193	44,664,613	Wisconsin	7,701	117,166,482	126,297,414	73,088,324	170,375
Missouri	10,281	121,601,812	185,477,432	80,939,500	226,139,744	Wyoming	448	3,085,890	7,766,446	3,068,242	7,784
						Totals	**582,996**	**6,755,223,402**	**9,923,615,779**	**4,727,298,568**	**11,951,540**

International students in the U.S. make a considerable contribution to local economies through tuition payments and cost of living expenditures.

1. 2001/2002 tuition, living, miscellaneous expenses from The College Board. These expenses are computed separately for undergraduate and graduate students and the sum of the two groups is reported here.
2. The number of spouses was estimated to be 85%, whose presence increases living expenses by 25%, and the number of children was estimated as six children for each group of ten couples in the U.S., whose presence increases expenses by 20%.

3. U.S. funding support level is computed based on the institution's Carnegie Type.

Analysis prepared for NAFSA by Lynn Schoch and Jason Baumgartner of Indiana University.

contributes nearly
the U. S. economy.

nternational students' presence in the U.S. is felt not just on campuses nationwide, but also on the U.S. economy locally and nationally. Student expenditures include tuition and cost of living expenses for themselves, and often expenses associated with their spouse and dependents who accompany them to the United States. The U.S. Department of Commerce ranked educational services as the nation's fifth largest service sector export in the year 2000, contributing almost $11 billion to the economy.

International students in the U.S. fund their education from a variety of sources. Many international graduate students, especially at Research Institutions, obtain research or teaching assistantships or other U.S.-based sources of funding. On the other hand, undergraduate internationals rely heavily on non-U.S. sources to fund their education. At Community Colleges, 91% of internationals have non-U.S. sources of funding for their education. This is not surprising, since community colleges are the most affordable of the different types of higher education institutions in the U.S., and rarely provide scholarships or assistantships. For international students in general, over two-thirds (68%) utilize personal and family sources as their primary source of funding. Undergraduate students have the largest percentage of personal funding for their U.S. studies (80.4%), while graduate students have a much smaller percentage of personal funding (51.5%).

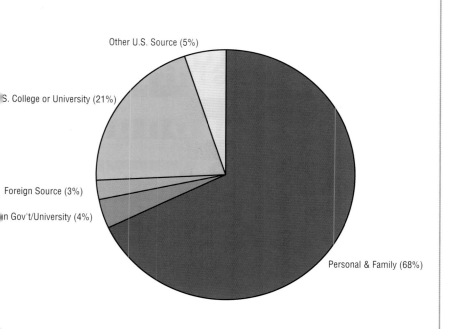

Other U.S. Source (5%)
S. College or University (21%)
Foreign Source (3%)
n Gov't/University (4%)
Personal & Family (68%)

Three-quarters of all international students have non-U.S. sources as the primary source of funding for their U.S. studies.

Primary Source of Funds	All Int'l Students	% of Under-graduate	% of Graduate	% of Other
Personal & Family	67.9	80.4	51.5	70.6
U.S. College or University	20.6	9.2	37.9	7.0
Home Government/University	3.7	3.5	3.9	3.6
U.S. Private Sponsor	2.7	3.5	1.8	1.9
Foreign Private Sponsor	2.0	2.2	1.9	1.8
Current Employment	1.9	0.2	1.5	13.7
Other Sources	0.2	0.2	0.2	0.4
U.S. Government	0.6	0.5	0.9	0.5
International Organization	0.3	0.2	0.5	0.5
Total Number of Students	**582,996**	**261,079**	**264,749**	**57,168**

80% of international undergraduate students are self-financed, while at the graduate level, half finance their own education.

India is the leading place of origin, with a 22.3% increase from the previous year and 11.5% of international students.

Rank	Place of Origin	2000/01	2001/02	2001/02 % Change	% of U.S. Int'l Student Total
	World Total	**547,867**	**582,996**	**6.4**	
1	India	54,664	66,836	22.3	11.5
2	China	59,939	63,211	5.5	10.8
3	Korea, Republic of	45,685	49,046	7.4	8.4
4	Japan	46,497	46,810	0.7	8.0
5	Taiwan	28,566	28,930	1.3	5.0
6	Canada	25,279	26,514	4.9	4.5
7	Mexico	10,670	12,518	17.3	2.1
8	Turkey	10,983	12,091	10.1	2.1
9	Indonesia	11,625	11,614	-0.1	2.0
10	Thailand	11,187	11,606	3.7	2.0
11	Germany	10,128	9,613	-5.1	1.6
12	Brazil	8,846	8,972	1.4	1.5
13	Pakistan	6,948	8,644	24.4	1.5
14	United Kingdom	8,139	8,414	3.4	1.4
15	Colombia	6,765	8,068	19.3	1.4

Nearly 44% of international students in the U.S. come from the top five places of origin, all of which are in Asia.

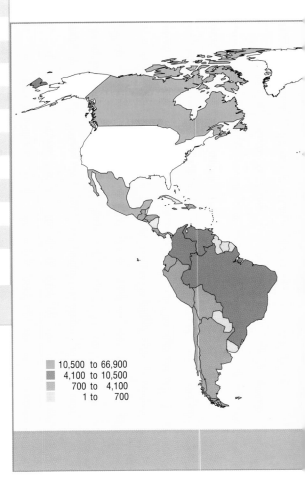

10,500 to 66,900
4,100 to 10,500
700 to 4,100
1 to 700

North America & Oceania (5%)

Africa (6%)

Middle East (7%)

America (12%)

Asia (56%)

Europe (14%)

Enrollments from Asia are more than double the enrollments from all of Europe and Latin America, the next largest regions of origin.

Seven of the fifteen leading places of origin are in Asia and 2001/2002 saw exceptional enrollment growth from China and India.

India has surpassed China as the leading place of origin for international students studying in the United States. The 66,836 Indian students represent a 22.3% increase from the previous year's total of 54,664. India's total represents 11.5% of the U.S. international student total enrollment. Other places of origin with large percentage increases in 2001/02 are Pakistan, (up 24.4% to 8,644), Colombia (up 19.3% to 8,068), Mexico (up 17.3% to 12,518), and Turkey (up 10.1% to 12,091). The leading places of origin in U.S. higher education vary by institutional type.

Fully 56% of international students are from Asia, as are the five leading places of origin. Two Asian places of origin ranked after India also have had large percentage increases: China ranked number two with a 5.5% increase, followed by Korea (up 7.4%). The majority of the Asian places of origin have economies that have begun to recover from the 1997 economic crisis. Of the Asian places of origin represented in the top 15 leading places of origin, only Indonesia's enrollments have decreased, reflecting its continuing economic slump.

Europe is the next leading region of origin, with 14% of total enrollment, followed by Latin America (12%), Middle East (7%), Africa (6%), and North America & Oceania (5%). Enrollments from Europe and North America & Oceania have declined slightly from the year before (down 1% each).

nations outside of Western Europe was 16.6% of total study abroad in 2000/01. Latin America has seen large gains, with numbers doubling since 1985/1986. Oceania's growth, from 0.9% to 6% in 2000/01, has been driven largely by study abroad to Australia.

Of the leading host countries, Australia, Italy, Greece, Spain, and Mexico saw the largest percent increases in 2000/01, all with double-digit increases. France, China, and Japan saw slight percent decreases in U.S. study abroad.

Western Europe continues to be the destination of choice for U.S. study abroad, but non-traditional destinations are attracting a growing number of students.

20|02 open**doors**

Over the past decade, the number of U.S. students studying abroad has more than doubled.

Scholars from China represent 18.2% of the 86,015 international scholars in the U.S.

Place of Origin	2000/01	2001/02	2001/02 % Change	% of U.S. Int'l Scholar Total
World Total	79,651	86,015	8.0	
China	14,772	15,624	5.8	18.2
Republic of Korea	5,830	7,143	22.5	8.3
India	5,456	6,249	14.5	7.3
Japan	5,905	5,736	-2.9	6.7
Germany	5,221	5,028	-3.7	5.8
Canada	3,735	3,905	4.6	4.5
United Kingdom	3,352	3,314	-1.1	3.9
Russia	3,253	3,123	-4.0	3.6
France	3,154	2,985	-5.4	3.5
Italy	2,226	2,257	1.4	2.6
Spain	1,706	1,822	6.8	2.1
Brazil	1,315	1,493	13.5	1.7
Australia	1,212	1,316	8.6	1.5
Taiwan	1,196	1,294	8.2	1.5
Israel	1,205	1,270	5.4	1.5
Turkey	918	1,141	24.3	1.3
Mexico	898	1,068	18.9	1.2
Netherlands	1,037	1,001	-3.5	1.2
Poland	862	980	13.7	1.1
Argentina	638	837	31.2	1.0

More than 18% of all international scholars in the U.S. come from China.

5,000 to 15,700
900 to 5,000
200 to 900
1 to 200

Leading Fields of Specialization	% of Scholars
Health Sciences	27.4
Life & Biological Sciences	14.6
Physical Sciences	14.0
Engineering	11.4
Social Sciences & History	4.5
Agriculture	3.4
Computer & Information Sciences	3.3
Business & Management	3.1
Mathematics	2.6
All Others	15.7
Total	**86,015**

The leading fields of specialization of international scholars are the sciences and engineering.

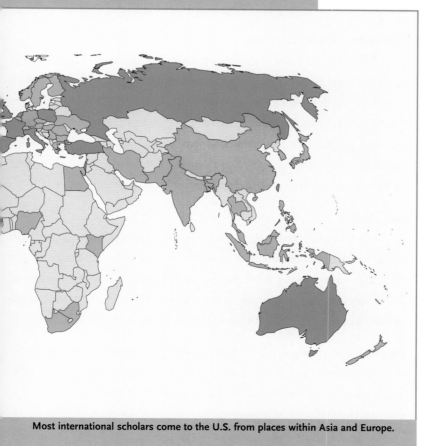

Most international scholars come to the U.S. from places within Asia and Europe.

8 6,015 international scholars conducted research or taught at U.S. higher education institutions in 2001/02. The 8% increase from 2000/01 builds on the previous six years' growth in scholar flows to the U.S. International scholars are highly concentrated at large research universities in the U.S. The majority of the scholars come from Asia and Europe. While European places of origin are more heavily represented among the leading 20 places of origin, there are more scholars from Asia in total. China is the leading place of origin of international scholars, with 18.2% (15,624) of the total scholars. This is an increase of 5.8% from previous year. The Republic of Korea is second, with 8.3% (7,143) of the total. Korean scholars' presence on U.S. campuses grew by 22.5% from previous year.

The international scholars are primarily involved in research activities in their fields of specialization. The majority of scholars are conducting research in the sciences. The leading field of specialization is the health sciences (27.4%), followed by life & biological sciences (14.6%), and physical sciences (14.0%). A large number are also involved in engineering (11.4%). A small percent of scholars are involved in teaching. Scholars are mainly male (69.3%), and most hold J visas.

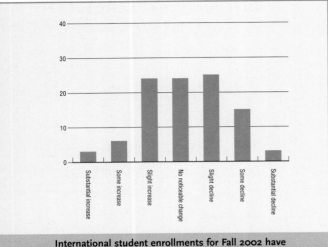

International student enrollments for Fall 2002 have remained level from the previous year.

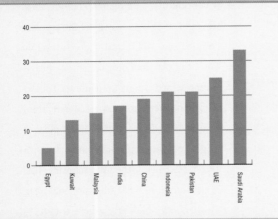

With the exception of Saudi Arabia and the UAE, there have been no substantial declines in international enrollments from most Islamic and other major sending countries.

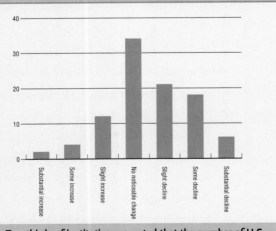

Two-thirds of institutions reported that the number of U.S. students abroad in Fall 2002 increased or remained level from last fall.

IMPACT OF SEPTEMBER 11, 2001 ON INTERNATIONAL EDUCATIONAL EXCHANGE: ONE YEAR LATER

n late October 2002, the Institute conducted an online survey through IIE Network, the Institute's membership website, in order to gauge the impact of September 11 on international educational exchange one year later. It was a follow-up to an initial online survey on this topic, sent out shortly after September 11, 2001. The survey was open to U.S. higher education institutions, including both Institute members and non-member institutions. Three hundred twenty-four educators, who identified themselves as representatives of mainly universities and four-year colleges, participated.

International Students

Respondents reported that international student enrollments appear stable and that there was no significant change in enrollments overall. Over half (57%), of the responding educators reported either increased or unchanged international enrollment in Fall 2002 compared to the same term last year. Although 42% of the respondents reported a decline, only 3% noted that it was a substantial decline (more than 30%).

Major Islamic Sending Countries

Respondents reported that they have not had substantial declines (more than 30%) in enrollments from most Islamic and other major sending countries, and that enrollments have been generally stable. Enrollments from Saudi Arabia and the United Arab Emirates may have been impacted the most. At least 80% of respondents reported that they have not seen a substantial drop in international student enrollments from most countries. Respondents suggested in an online discussion board that visa delays or denial, financial issues, or the preference for other host countries might be contributing factors.

Study Abroad

Respondents suggested that study abroad by American students is more popular than ever in the current academic year. Over two-thirds of respondents noted that the number of students studying abroad in Fall 2002 had either continued to increase or remained level on their campus compared to the same term last year. 30% of the respondents noted that they have seen an increase in U.S. study abroad in non-traditional destinations.

All of these findings support feedback and anecdotal information from educators that the events of September 11 have raised student awareness of world affairs. American students continue to seek opportunities to study abroad, and international students are continuing to come to the United States to study despite the terrible events of September 11.

For a full survey report, please go to http://opendoors.iienetwork.org.

INTERNATIONAL STUDENTS

Place of Origin	2000/01	2001/02	% Change	Place of Origin	2000/01	2001/02	% Change
AFRICA	**34,217**	**37,724**	**10.2**	**Southern Africa**	**3,304**	**3,443**	**4.2**
Africa, Unspecified	8	0	-100.0	Botswana	941	1,004	6.7
				Lesotho	35	39	11.4
East Africa	**13,516**	**15,331**	**13.4**	Namibia	117	80	-31.6
Burundi	55	75	36.4	South Africa	2,106	2,232	6.0
Comoros	38	44	15.8	Swaziland	104	88	-15.4
Djibouti	8	8	0.0	Southern Africa, Unspecified	1	0	-100.0
Eritrea	134	161	20.1				
Ethiopia	1,205	1,133	-6.0	**West Africa**	**10,346**	**11,385**	**10.0**
Kenya	6,229	7,097	13.9	Benin	145	153	5.5
Madagascar	115	124	7.8	Burkina Faso	112	135	20.5
Malawi	428	475	11.0	Cape Verde	59	57	-3.4
Mauritius	246	251	2.0	Côte d'Ivoire	637	707	11.0
Mozambique	86	106	23.3	Gambia	386	401	3.9
Reunion	2	20	900.0	Ghana	2,469	2,672	8.2
Rwanda	261	263	0.8	Guinea	237	220	-7.2
Seychelles	13	20	53.8	Guinea-Bissau	16	21	31.3
Somalia	96	87	-9.4	Liberia	451	471	4.4
Tanzania	1,528	1,814	18.7	Mali	439	311	-29.2
Uganda	754	805	6.8	Mauritania	73	79	8.2
Zambia	613	819	33.6	Niger	87	139	59.8
Zimbabwe	1,703	2,029	19.1	Nigeria	3,820	4,499	17.8
East Africa, Unspecified	2	0	-100.0	Senegal	732	809	10.5
				Sierra Leone	336	320	-4.8
Central Africa	**1,859**	**1,972**	**6.1**	St. Helena	1	1	0.0
Angola	348	360	3.4	Togo	330	382	15.8
Cameroon	870	967	11.1	West Africa, Unspecified	16	8	-50.0
Central African Republic	18	12	-33.3				
Chad	51	60	17.6	**ASIA**	**302,058**	**324,812**	**7.5**
Congo	0	8	-	Asia, Unspecified	6	0	-100.0
Equatorial Guinea	44	35	-20.5				
Gabon	98	101	3.1	**East Asia**	**189,371**	**196,813**	**3.9**
São Tomé & Príncipe	13	7	-46.2	China	59,939	63,211	5.5
Zaire/Congo	411	422	2.7	Hong Kong	7,627	7,757	1.7
Central Africa, Unspecified	6	0	-100.0	Japan	46,497	46,810	0.7
				Korea, Dem. People's Rep.	127	113	-11.0
North Africa	**5,184**	**5,593**	**7.9**	Korea, Republic of	45,685	49,046	7.4
Algeria	220	196	-10.9	Macao	372	371	-0.3
Egypt	2,255	2,409	6.8	Mongolia	442	574	29.9
Libya	39	42	7.7	Taiwan	28,566	28,930	1.3
Morocco	1,917	2,102	9.7	East Asia, Unspecified	116	1	-99.1
Sudan	366	378	3.3				
Tunisia	385	458	19.0	**South & Central Asia**	**71,765**	**86,131**	**20.0**
Western Sahara	2	8	300.0	Afghanistan	75	92	22.7
				Bangladesh	4,114	3,935	-4.4
				Bhutan	62	78	25.8

1   **INTERNATIONAL STUDENT TOTALS BY PLACE OF ORIGIN, 2000/01 & 2001/02**

Place of Origin	2000/01	2001/02	% Change	Place of Origin	2000/01	2001/02	% Change
India	54,664	66,836	22.3	**Eastern Europe**	**27,674**	**29,591**	**6.9**
Kazakhstan	540	617	14.3	Albania	1,118	1,129	1.0
Kyrgyzstan	160	230	43.8	Armenia	366	439	19.9
Nepal	2,618	3,019	15.3	Azerbaijan	253	277	9.5
Pakistan	6,948	8,644	24.4	Belarus	311	411	32.2
Republic of Maldives	13	16	23.1	Bosnia & Herzegovina	477	511	7.1
Sri Lanka	1,964	2,069	5.3	Bulgaria	3,270	3,584	9.6
Tajikistan	118	143	21.2	Croatia	782	802	2.6
Turkmenistan	65	71	9.2	Czech Republic	1,112	1,152	3.6
Uzbekistan	418	381	-8.9	Czechoslovakia, Former	39	11	-71.8
South Asia, Unspecified	6	0	-100.0	Estonia	287	293	2.1
				Georgia	329	345	4.9
Southeast Asia	**40,916**	**41,868**	**2.3**	Hungary	1,174	1,242	5.8
Brunei	25	27	8.0	Latvia	383	434	13.3
Cambodia	187	247	32.1	Lithuania	493	628	27.4
East Timor	0	4	-	Macedonia	281	337	19.9
Indonesia	11,625	11,614	-0.1	Moldova	183	269	47.0
Laos	96	133	38.5	Poland	2,432	2,606	7.2
Malaysia	7,795	7,395	-5.1	Romania	2,976	3,325	11.7
Myanmar	673	875	30.0	Russia	6,858	6,643	-3.1
Philippines	3,139	3,295	5.0	Slovakia	539	627	16.3
Singapore	4,166	4,141	-0.6	Slovenia	207	225	8.7
Thailand	11,187	11,606	3.7	Ukraine	1,909	2,195	15.0
Vietnam	2,022	2,531	25.2	U.S.S.R., Former	105	79	-24.8
Southeast Asia, Unspecified	1	0	-100.0	Yugoslavia, Former	1,790	2,027	13.2
MIDDLE EAST	**36,858**	**38,545**	**4.6**	**Western Europe**	**52,910**	**51,988**	**-1.7**
Bahrain	562	601	6.9	Andorra	5	8	60.0
Cyprus	2,217	2,027	-8.6	Austria	1,062	1,079	1.6
Iran	1,844	2,216	20.2	Belgium	881	884	0.3
Iraq	155	147	-5.2	Denmark	1,007	922	-8.4
Israel	3,402	3,458	1.6	Finland	893	819	-8.3
Jordan	2,187	2,417	10.5	France	7,273	7,401	1.8
Kuwait	3,045	2,966	-2.6	Germany	10,128	9,613	-5.1
Lebanon	2,005	2,435	21.4	Gibraltar	4	1	-75.0
Oman	702	623	-11.3	Greece	2,768	2,599	-6.1
Palestinian Authority	237	232	-2.1	Iceland	558	891	59.7
Qatar	463	461	-0.4	Ireland	1,086	1,053	-3.0
Saudi Arabia	5,273	5,579	5.8	Italy	3,490	3,333	-4.5
Syria	713	735	3.1	Liechtenstein	13	12	-7.7
Turkey	10,983	12,091	10.1	Luxembourg	73	61	-16.4
United Arab Emirates	2,659	2,121	-20.2	Malta	61	51	-16.4
Yemen	411	436	6.1	Monaco	18	15	-16.7
				Netherlands	1,856	1,791	-3.5
EUROPE	**80,584**	**81,579**	**1.2**	Norway	2,098	2,323	10.7
				Portugal	884	946	7.0

1   (cont'd) INTERNATIONAL STUDENT TOTALS BY PLACE OF ORIGIN, 2000/01 & 2001/02

Place of Origin	2000/01	2001/02	% Change	Place of Origin	2000/01	2001/02	% Change
San Marino	4	2	-50.0	**South America**	**32,447**	**35,653**	**9.9**
Spain	4,156	4,048	-2.6	Argentina	3,172	3,444	8.6
Sweden	4,598	4,041	-12.1	Bolivia	897	953	6.2
Switzerland	1,850	1,680	-9.2	Brazil	8,846	8,972	1.4
United Kingdom	8,139	8,414	3.4	Chile	1,553	1,655	6.6
Vatican City	5	1	-80.0	Colombia	6,765	8,068	19.3
				Ecuador	2,028	2,364	16.6
LATIN AMERICA	**63,634**	**68,358**	**7.4**	Falkland Islands	4	1	-75.0
				French Guiana	5	6	20.0
Caribbean	**14,423**	**13,879**	**-3.8**	Guyana	409	359	-12.2
Anguilla	65	46	-29.2	Paraguay	371	375	1.1
Antigua	271	239	-11.8	Peru	2,660	3,188	19.8
Aruba	85	64	-24.7	Suriname	121	100	-17.4
Bahamas	1,762	1,973	12.0	Uruguay	397	468	17.9
Barbados	647	580	-10.4	Venezuela	5,217	5,627	7.9
British Virgin Islands	84	97	15.5	South America, Unspecified	2	73	3,550.0
Cayman Islands	243	211	-13.2				
Cuba	517	163	-68.5	**NORTH AMERICA**	**25,888**	**27,039**	**4.4**
Dominica	258	232	-10.1	Bermuda	609	525	-13.8
Dominican Republic	869	898	3.3	Canada	25,279	26,514	4.9
Grenada	281	185	-34.2				
Guadeloupe	10	8	-20.0	**OCEANIA**	**4,624**	**4,852**	**4.9**
Haiti	1,012	1,184	17.0	Australia	2,645	2,707	2.3
Jamaica	4,225	4,286	1.4	Cook Islands	4	4	0.0
Martinique	8	13	62.5	Fed. States of Micronesia	188	274	45.7
Montserrat	10	6	-40.0	Fiji	250	247	-1.2
Netherlands Antilles	352	335	-4.8	French Polynesia	71	110	54.9
St. Kitts-Nevis	271	146	-46.1	Kiribati	42	35	-16.7
St. Lucia	267	269	0.7	Marshall Islands	37	40	8.1
St. Vincent	139	131	-5.8	Nauru	4	2	-50.0
Trinidad & Tobago	2,901	2,668	-8.0	New Caledonia	7	2	-71.4
Turks & Caicos Islands	48	64	33.3	New Zealand	971	1,046	7.7
Windward Islands	1	0	-100.0	Niue	5	18	260.0
Caribbean, Unspecified	97	81	-16.5	Norfolk Island	1	2	100.0
				Palau	48	45	-6.3
Central America/Mexico	**16,764**	**18,826**	**12.3**	Papua New Guinea	30	32	6.7
Belize	489	542	10.8	Solomon Islands	7	8	14.3
Costa Rica	928	966	4.1	Tonga	188	164	-12.8
El Salvador	825	917	11.2	Tuvalu	2	2	0.0
Guatemala	1,050	1,058	0.8	Vanuatu	5	6	20.0
Honduras	974	1,007	3.4	Western Samoa	118	107	-9.3
Mexico	10,670	12,518	17.3	Pacific Islands, Unspecified	1	1	0.0
Nicaragua	611	608	-0.5				
Panama	1,217	1,208	-0.7	**STATELESS**	**10**	**87**	**770.0**
Cent. Am. & Mexico, Unspec.	0	2	-				
				WORLD TOTAL	**547,867**	**582,996**	**6.4**

1 (cont'd) INTERNATIONAL STUDENT TOTALS BY PLACE OF ORIGIN, 2000/01 & 2001/02

Place of Origin	Under-graduate	% Under-graduate	Graduate	% Graduate	Other	% Other	Total
AFRICA	**25,197**	**66.8**	**10,836**	**28.7**	**1,701**	**4.5**	**37,724**
East Africa	**11,172**	**72.9**	**3,717**	**24.2**	**441**	**2.9**	**15,331**
Burundi	67	88.3	8	10.0	1	1.7	75
Comoros	13	29.7	6	13.5	25	56.8	44
Djibouti	6	71.4	1	14.3	1	14.3	8
Eritrea	55	34.1	100	61.9	6	4.0	161
Ethiopia	757	66.8	340	30.0	36	3.2	1,133
Kenya	5,268	74.2	1,654	23.3	175	2.5	7,097
Madagascar	46	37.0	71	57.0	7	6.0	124
Malawi	331	69.8	134	28.1	10	2.0	475
Mauritius	165	65.7	74	29.5	12	4.8	251
Mozambique	47	44.2	47	44.2	12	11.6	106
Reunion	19	94.1	1	5.9	0	0.0	20
Rwanda	200	76.1	57	21.6	6	2.3	263
Seychelles	18	88.2	2	11.8	0	0.0	20
Somalia	68	78.6	16	18.6	2	2.9	87
Tanzania	1,417	78.1	340	18.7	57	3.1	1,814
Uganda	465	57.8	307	38.1	32	4.0	805
Zambia	617	75.3	184	22.5	18	2.2	819
Zimbabwe	1,613	79.5	375	18.5	41	2.0	2,029
Central Africa	**1,457**	**73.9**	**390**	**19.8**	**130**	**6.6**	**1,972**
Angola	304	84.5	28	7.8	28	7.8	360
Cameroon	675	69.8	253	26.1	40	4.1	967
Central African Republic	7	60.0	4	30.0	1	10.0	12
Chad	41	68.0	10	16.0	10	16.0	60
Congo	6	71.4	2	28.6	0	0.0	8
Equatorial Guinea	25	70.0	4	10.0	7	20.0	35
Gabon	73	71.6	20	19.8	9	8.6	101
São Tomé & Príncipe	2	33.3	5	66.7	0	0.0	7
Zaire/Congo	324	76.7	64	15.1	35	8.2	422
North Africa	**2,582**	**46.2**	**2,597**	**46.4**	**416**	**7.4**	**5,593**
Algeria	90	45.9	90	45.9	16	8.2	196
Egypt	765	31.7	1,501	62.3	144	6.0	2,409
Libya	20	47.2	16	38.9	6	13.9	42
Morocco	1,283	61.1	642	30.6	176	8.4	2,102
Sudan	190	50.3	156	41.1	32	8.5	378
Tunisia	229	50.0	188	40.9	42	9.1	458
Western Sahara	5	57.1	4	42.9	0	0.0	8
Southern Africa	**2,276**	**66.1**	**1,032**	**30.0**	**136**	**4.0**	**3,443**
Botswana	777	77.4	201	20.1	25	2.5	1,004

Place of Origin	Under-graduate	% Under-graduate	Graduate	% Graduate	Other	% Other	Total
Lesotho	20	51.7	16	41.4	3	6.9	39
Namibia	52	64.6	27	33.8	1	1.5	80
South Africa	1,367	61.2	764	34.2	102	4.6	2,232
Swaziland	60	67.6	24	27.0	5	5.4	88
West Africa	**7,710**	**67.7**	**3,100**	**27.2**	**578**	**5.1**	**11,385**
Benin	83	54.0	62	40.5	9	5.6	153
Burkina Faso	67	49.1	48	35.5	21	15.5	135
Cape Verde	47	83.3	8	14.6	1	2.1	57
Côte d'Ivoire	495	70.0	139	19.6	74	10.4	707
Gambia	352	87.8	39	9.9	10	2.4	401
Ghana	1,639	61.3	937	35.1	96	3.6	2,672
Guinea	160	72.6	27	12.4	33	15.1	220
Guinea-Bissau	16	77.8	5	22.2	0	0.0	21
Liberia	374	79.4	83	17.6	14	3.1	471
Mali	198	63.8	76	24.4	37	11.8	311
Mauritania	53	67.2	11	13.4	15	19.4	79
Niger	82	59.0	39	28.2	18	12.8	139
Nigeria	3,059	68.0	1,308	29.1	132	2.9	4,499
Senegal	585	72.2	164	20.2	61	7.5	809
Sierra Leone	226	70.6	91	28.3	4	1.1	320
St. Helena	0	0.0	1	100.0	0	0.0	1
Togo	266	69.7	62	16.3	53	14.0	382
West Africa, Unspecified	8	100.0	0	0.0	0	0.0	8
ASIA	**125,842**	**38.7**	**174,670**	**53.8**	**24,299**	**7.5**	**324,812**
East Asia	**76,556**	**38.9**	**102,128**	**51.9**	**18,130**	**9.2**	**196,813**
China	8,659	13.7	50,969	80.6	3,583	5.7	63,211
Hong Kong	5,840	75.3	1,515	19.5	402	5.2	7,757
Japan	31,588	67.5	9,691	20.7	5,531	11.8	46,810
Korea, Dem. People's Rep.	58	51.6	45	40.0	10	8.4	113
Korea, Republic of	19,786	40.3	23,676	48.3	5,585	11.4	49,046
Macao	269	72.4	76	20.5	26	7.1	371
Mongolia	271	47.3	232	40.5	70	12.2	574
Taiwan	10,085	34.9	15,923	55.0	2,923	10.1	28,930
East Asia, Unspecified	0	0.0	1	100.0	0	0.0	1
South & Central Asia	**26,028**	**30.2**	**56,585**	**65.7**	**3,516**	**4.1**	**86,131**
Afghanistan	75	82.1	13	14.1	4	3.8	92
Bangladesh	2,191	55.7	1,621	41.2	123	3.1	3,935
Bhutan	49	63.1	24	30.8	5	6.2	78
India	14,321	21.4	49,730	74.4	2,785	4.2	66,836
Kazakhstan	291	47.1	278	45.1	48	7.8	617

2   (cont'd) INTERNATIONAL STUDENTS BY ACADEMIC LEVEL AND PLACE OF ORIGIN, 2001/02

Place of Origin	Under-graduate	% Under-graduate	Graduate	% Graduate	Other	% Other	Total
Kyrgyzstan	109	47.4	98	42.7	23	9.9	230
Nepal	2,141	70.9	776	25.7	103	3.4	3,019
Pakistan	5,368	62.1	2,961	34.3	314	3.6	8,644
Republic of Maldives	9	53.8	5	30.8	3	15.4	16
Sri Lanka	1,155	55.9	850	41.1	63	3.1	2,069
Tajikistan	100	70.5	31	21.9	11	7.6	143
Turkmenistan	36	50.8	31	44.1	4	5.1	71
Uzbekistan	183	48.2	167	44.0	30	7.8	381
Southeast Asia	**23,258**	**55.6**	**15,957**	**38.1**	**2,653**	**6.3**	**41,868**
Brunei	16	59.1	10	36.4	1	4.5	27
Cambodia	172	69.4	50	20.4	25	10.2	247
East Timor	1	33.3	2	66.7	0	0.0	4
Indonesia	8,083	69.6	2,827	24.3	704	6.1	11,614
Laos	93	69.7	32	24.2	8	6.1	133
Malaysia	5,121	69.2	1,927	26.1	347	4.7	7,395
Myanmar	720	82.2	133	15.2	22	2.5	875
Philippines	1,880	57.0	1,251	38.0	165	5.0	3,295
Singapore	2,440	58.9	1,490	36.0	211	5.1	4,141
Thailand	2,880	24.8	7,672	66.1	1,055	9.1	11,606
Vietnam	1,852	73.2	563	22.2	115	4.6	2,531
MIDDLE EAST	**19,032**	**49.4**	**16,347**	**42.4**	**3,165**	**8.2**	**38,545**
Bahrain	453	75.4	121	20.2	26	4.4	601
Cyprus	1,287	63.5	661	32.6	79	3.9	2,027
Iran	796	35.9	1,295	58.5	124	5.6	2,216
Iraq	84	56.8	55	37.6	8	5.6	147
Israel	1,580	45.7	1,666	48.2	212	6.1	3,458
Jordan	1,068	44.2	1,211	50.1	138	5.7	2,417
Kuwait	2,239	75.5	565	19.0	163	5.5	2,966
Lebanon	1,358	55.8	947	38.9	129	5.3	2,435
Oman	414	66.4	174	27.9	36	5.7	623
Palestinian Authority	112	48.1	101	43.4	20	8.5	232
Qatar	346	75.1	67	14.5	48	10.4	461
Saudi Arabia	3,080	55.2	1,775	31.8	724	13.0	5,579
Syria	343	46.7	287	39.0	106	14.4	735
Turkey	3,804	31.5	7,106	58.8	1,180	9.8	12,091
United Arab Emirates	1,764	83.2	225	10.6	132	6.2	2,121
Yemen	304	69.8	91	21.0	40	9.3	436
EUROPE	**40,611**	**49.8**	**34,268**	**42.0**	**6,693**	**8.2**	**81,579**
Eastern Europe	14,855	50.2	13,012	44.0	1,721	5.8	29,591
Albania	805	71.3	277	24.5	47	4.1	1,129

2   (cont'd) INTERNATIONAL STUDENTS BY ACADEMIC LEVEL AND PLACE OF ORIGIN, 2001/02

Place of Origin	Under- graduate	% Under- graduate	Graduate	% Graduate	Other	% Other	Total
Armenia	152	34.5	262	59.7	25	5.8	439
Azerbaijan	92	33.3	160	57.8	25	8.9	277
Belarus	224	54.5	163	39.6	24	6.0	411
Bosnia & Herzegovina	363	70.9	128	25.1	21	4.0	511
Bulgaria	2,129	59.4	1,289	36.0	165	4.6	3,584
Croatia	432	53.9	330	41.2	40	4.9	802
Czech Republic	700	60.7	386	33.5	66	5.7	1,152
Czechoslovakia, Former	9	88.9	1	11.1	0	0.0	11
Estonia	196	66.8	84	28.7	13	4.5	293
Georgia	142	41.3	181	52.4	22	6.3	345
Hungary	624	50.3	542	43.7	75	6.0	1,242
Latvia	275	63.4	130	29.9	29	6.6	434
Lithuania	378	60.2	210	33.5	40	6.3	628
Macedonia	218	64.8	101	29.9	18	5.3	337
Moldova	152	56.4	96	35.8	21	7.8	269
Poland	1,618	62.1	784	30.1	203	7.8	2,606
Romania	957	28.8	2,214	66.6	154	4.6	3,325
Russia	2,843	42.8	3,380	50.9	421	6.3	6,643
Slovakia	367	58.6	206	32.9	53	8.5	627
Slovenia	120	53.2	92	41.0	13	5.9	225
U.S.S.R., Former	51	64.2	27	34.3	1	1.5	79
Ukraine	915	41.7	1,117	50.9	162	7.4	2,195
Yugoslavia, Former	1,093	53.9	852	42.0	83	4.1	2,027
Western Europe	**25,756**	**49.5**	**21,256**	**40.9**	**4,972**	**9.6**	**51,988**
Andorra	6	71.4	2	28.6	0	0.0	8
Austria	546	50.6	395	36.6	138	12.8	1,079
Belgium	420	47.5	391	44.3	72	8.2	884
Denmark	428	46.4	360	39.0	134	14.6	922
Finland	540	66.0	221	27.0	57	7.0	819
France	3,195	43.2	3,258	44.0	947	12.8	7,401
Germany	4,368	45.4	4,256	44.3	989	10.3	9,613
Gibraltar	1	100.0	0	0.0	0	0.0	1
Greece	844	32.5	1,629	62.7	126	4.8	2,599
Iceland	285	32.0	566	63.6	39	4.4	891
Ireland	528	50.1	443	42.1	82	7.8	1,053
Italy	1,091	32.7	1,920	57.6	322	9.7	3,333
Liechtenstein	8	70.0	2	20.0	1	10.0	12
Luxembourg	33	53.8	27	44.2	1	1.9	61
Malta	19	38.1	28	54.8	4	7.1	51
Monaco	9	61.5	4	23.1	2	15.4	15
Netherlands	926	51.7	670	37.4	194	10.9	1,791
Norway	1,608	69.2	566	24.3	150	6.5	2,323
Portugal	451	47.6	451	47.6	44	4.7	946

2   (cont'd) INTERNATIONAL STUDENTS BY ACADEMIC LEVEL AND PLACE OF ORIGIN, 2001/02

Place of Origin	Under-graduate	% Under-graduate	Graduate	% Graduate	Other	% Other	Total
San Marino	0	0.0	2	100.0	0	0.0	2
Spain	1,655	40.9	1,990	49.2	403	9.9	4,048
Sweden	3,037	75.1	701	17.3	304	7.5	4,041
Switzerland	818	48.7	658	39.2	204	12.1	1,680
United Kingdom	4,939	58.7	2,716	32.3	759	9.0	8,414
Vatican City	1	100.0	0	0.0	0	0.0	1
LATIN AMERICA	**41,595**	**60.8**	**21,759**	**31.8**	**5,002**	**7.3**	**68,358**
Caribbean	**10,660**	**76.8**	**2,879**	**20.7**	**336**	**2.4**	**13,879**
Anguilla	42	92.3	4	7.7	0	0.0	46
Antigua	177	73.9	55	23.1	7	3.0	239
Aruba	57	90.4	5	7.7	1	1.9	64
Bahamas	1,612	81.7	328	16.6	33	1.7	1,973
Barbados	393	67.8	161	27.8	25	4.4	580
British Virgin Islands	77	80.0	13	13.8	6	6.3	97
Cayman Islands	185	87.5	24	11.2	3	1.3	211
Cuba	110	67.6	47	28.7	6	3.7	163
Dominica	172	74.0	56	24.0	5	2.1	232
Dominican Republic	596	66.4	241	26.9	60	6.7	898
Grenada	128	69.4	49	26.8	7	3.8	185
Guadeloupe	5	57.1	4	42.9	0	0.0	8
Haiti	1,002	84.6	164	13.9	18	1.5	1,184
Jamaica	3,297	76.9	917	21.4	73	1.7	4,286
Martinique	11	81.8	1	9.1	1	9.1	13
Montserrat	5	80.0	1	20.0	0	0.0	6
Netherlands Antilles	267	79.8	53	16.0	14	4.3	335
St. Kitts-Nevis	89	60.9	52	35.7	5	3.5	146
St. Lucia	206	76.7	55	20.6	7	2.7	269
St. Vincent	90	68.5	40	30.6	1	0.9	131
Trinidad & Tobago	2,013	75.4	594	22.3	61	2.3	2,668
Turks & Caicos Islands	54	84.9	8	13.2	1	1.9	64
Caribbean, Unspecified	72	88.1	7	9.0	2	3.0	81
Central America/Mexico	**11,876**	**63.1**	**5,845**	**31.0**	**1,105**	**5.9**	**18,826**
Belize	403	74.5	115	21.2	24	4.4	542
Costa Rica	528	54.6	397	41.1	41	4.3	966
El Salvador	735	80.2	137	14.9	45	4.9	917
Guatemala	779	73.6	235	22.2	44	4.2	1,058
Honduras	748	74.2	200	19.9	59	5.9	1,007
Mexico	7,345	58.7	4,389	35.1	784	6.3	12,518
Nicaragua	481	79.1	97	16.0	30	4.9	608
Panama	857	71.0	274	22.7	77	6.4	1,208
Cent. Am. & Mexico, Unspec.	0	0.0	1	50.0	1	50.0	2

2   (cont'd) INTERNATIONAL STUDENTS BY ACADEMIC LEVEL AND PLACE OF ORIGIN, 2001/02

Place of Origin	Under-graduate	% Under-graduate	Graduate	% Graduate	Other	% Other	Total
South America	**19,059**	**53.5**	**13,035**	**36.6**	**3,561**	**10.0**	**35,653**
Argentina	1,381	40.1	1,797	52.2	266	7.7	3,444
Bolivia	648	67.9	252	26.5	53	5.6	953
Brazil	4,921	54.8	3,271	36.5	781	8.7	8,972
Chile	569	34.4	901	54.5	185	11.2	1,655
Colombia	4,399	54.5	2,789	34.6	880	10.9	8,068
Ecuador	1,564	66.1	600	25.4	201	8.5	2,364
Falkland Islands	1	100.0	0	0.0	0	0.0	1
French Guiana	6	100.0	0	0.0	0	0.0	6
Guyana	249	69.4	101	28.2	8	2.3	359
Paraguay	252	67.2	85	22.6	38	10.2	375
Peru	1,664	52.2	1,256	39.4	269	8.4	3,188
Suriname	73	72.6	24	23.8	4	3.6	100
Uruguay	207	44.2	230	49.2	31	6.5	468
Venezuela	3,053	54.3	1,728	30.7	845	15.0	5,627
South America, Unspecified	72	98.4	1	1.6	0	0.0	73
NORTH AMERICA	**13,891**	**51.4**	**11,906**	**44.0**	**1,244**	**4.6**	**27,039**
Bermuda	419	79.7	96	18.3	11	2.1	525
Canada	13,472	50.8	11,810	44.5	1,233	4.6	26,514
OCEANIA	**2,940**	**60.6**	**1,663**	**34.3**	**249**	**5.1**	**4,852**
Australia	1,499	55.4	1,042	38.5	167	6.2	2,707
Cook Islands	2	66.7	1	33.3	0	0.0	4
Fed. States of Micronesia	257	93.8	6	2.2	11	4.0	274
Fiji	215	87.1	28	11.5	4	1.4	247
French Polynesia	105	95.7	4	3.2	1	1.1	110
Kiribati	27	76.7	7	20.0	1	3.3	35
Marshall Islands	37	91.2	2	5.9	1	2.9	40
Nauru	2	100.0	0	0.0	0	0.0	2
New Caledonia	1	50.0	1	50.0	0	0.0	2
New Zealand	457	43.7	528	50.5	60	5.8	1,046
Niue	15	85.7	3	14.3	0	0.0	18
Norfolk Island	2	100.0	0	0.0	0	0.0	2
Palau	44	97.4	1	2.6	0	0.0	45
Papua New Guinea	23	72.0	8	24.0	1	4.0	32
Solomon Islands	5	57.1	4	42.9	0	0.0	8
Tonga	143	87.1	19	11.5	2	1.4	164
Tuvalu	1	50.0	1	50.0	0	0.0	2
Vanuatu	4	60.0	2	40.0	0	0.0	6
Western Samoa	101	94.5	6	5.5	0	0.0	107
Pacific Islands, Unspecified	0	0.0	0	0.0	1	100.0	1

2   (cont'd) INTERNATIONAL STUDENTS BY ACADEMIC LEVEL AND PLACE OF ORIGIN, 2001/02

Place of Origin	Under-graduate	% Under-graduate	Graduate	% Graduate	Other	% Other	Total
STATELESS	32	36.5	52	59.5	4	4.1	87
WORLD TOTAL	269,446	46.2	271,182	46.5	42,368	7.3	582,996

2 (cont'd) INTERNATIONAL STUDENTS BY ACADEMIC LEVEL AND PLACE OF ORIGIN, 2001/02

Rank	Metropolitan Statistical Area	Number of Int'l Students	Rank	Metropolitan Statistical Area	Number of Int'l Students
1	New York, NY	35,737	28	Honolulu, HI	4,991
2	Los Angeles-Long Beach, CA	28,573	29	Oklahoma City, OK	4,893
3	Boston, MA-NH	24,117	30	Lafayette, IN	4,728
4	Washington, DC-MD-VA-WV	21,727	31	Newark, NJ	4,704
5	Chicago, IL	16,170	32	Champaign-Urbana, IL	4,662
6	Philadelphia, PA-NJ	11,002	33	St. Louis, MO-IL	4,557
7	Houston, TX	10,561	34	Gainesville, FL	4,375
8	Dallas, TX	9,390	35	Tampa-St. Petersburg-Clearwater, FL	3,979
9	San Jose, CA	9,250	36	Madison, WI	3,870
10	San Francisco, CA	8,375	37	State College, PA	3,847
Total of top 10		**174,902**	38	Tucson, AZ	3,627
			39	Denver, CO	3,624
11	Miami, FL	8,117	40	Bryan-College Station, TX	3,563
12	Atlanta, GA	8,075	41	Lansing-East Lansing, MI	3,512
13	Seattle-Bellevue-Everett, WA	7,674	42	Providence-Fall River-Warwick, RI-MA	3,378
14	Phoenix-Mesa, AZ	6,463	43	Middlesex-Somerset-Hunterdon, NJ	3,371
15	Oakland, CA	6,423	44	Bloomington, IN	3,344
16	San Diego, CA	6,308	45	Fort Worth-Arlington, TX	3,289
17	Austin-San Marcos, TX	6,298	46	Riverside-San Bernardino, CA	3,198
18	Detroit, MI	6,289	47	Rochester, NY	3,122
19	Orange County, CA	6,182	48	Cleveland-Lorain-Elyria, OH	2,961
20	Ann Arbor, MI	6,017	49	Springfield, MA	2,905
21	Columbus, OH	5,814	50	Hartford, CT	2,900
22	Pittsburgh, PA	5,753	51	El Paso, TX	2,688
23	Baltimore, MD	5,665	52	Orlando, FL	2,672
24	Buffalo-Niagara Falls, NY	5,648	53	Syracuse, NY	2,580
25	Minneapolis-St.Paul, MN-WI	5,559	54	Portland-Vancouver, OR-WA	2,463
26	Raleigh-Durham-Chapel Hill, NC	5,396	55	Provo-Orem, UT	2,433
27	Nassau-Suffolk, NY	5,122	56	Salt Lake City-Ogden, UT	2,426

3 INTERNATIONAL ENROLLMENTS IN MSAs WITH MORE THAN 1,000 INTERNATIONAL STUDENTS, 2001/02

Rank	Metropolitan Statistical Area	Number of Int'l Students	Rank	Metropolitan Statistical Area	Number of Int'l Students
57	Cincinnati, OH-KY-IN	2,391	87	Trenton, NJ	1,466
58	New Haven-Meriden, CT	2,362	88	Columbia, MO	1,438
59	Albany-Schenectady-Troy, NY	2,354	89	Athens, GA	1,437
60	West Palm Beach-Boca Raton, FL	2,337	90	Charlotte-Gastonia-Rock Hill, NC-SC	1,414
61	New Orleans, LA	2,257	91	Charlottesville, VA	1,410
62	Kalamazoo-Battle Creek, MI	2,244	92	Sacramento, CA	1,371
63	Wichita, KS	2,201	93	Tallahassee, FL	1,288
64	Kansas City, MO-KS	2,108	94	Tulsa, OK	1,277
65	Eugene-Springfield, OR	2,067	95	South Bend, IN	1,275
66	Iowa City, IA	2,027	96	Worcester, MA-CT	1,257
67	Norfolk-Virginia Beach-Newport News, VA-NC	1,992	97	Indianapolis, IN	1,250
68	Bergen-Passaic, NJ	1,971	98	Daytona Beach, FL	1,241
69	Lexington, KY	1,938	99	Birmingham, AL	1,230
70	Baton Rouge, LA	1,937	99	Memphis, TN-AR-MS	1,230
71	Toledo, OH	1,936	101	Corvallis, OR	1,217
72	Milwaukee-Waukesha, WI	1,903	102	Reno, NV	1,216
73	Bridgeport, CT	1,829	103	Greensboro-Winston-Salem-High Point, NC	1,186
74	Omaha, NE-IA	1,786	104	Boulder-Longmont, CO	1,164
75	Fort Lauderdale, FL	1,697	105	Fresno, CA	1,163
75	Wilmington-Newark, DE-MD	1,697	106	Knoxville, TN	1,147
77	Lawrence, KS	1,687	107	Binghamton, NY	1,143
78	Nashville, TN	1,656	108	Fayetteville-Springdale-Rogers, AR	1,127
79	San Antonio, TX	1,650	109	Greenville-Spartanburg-Anderson, SC	1,122
80	Akron, OH	1,645	110	Melbourne-Titusville-Palm Bay, FL	1,107
81	Las Vegas, NV-AZ	1,642	111	Richmond-Petersburg, VA	1,075
82	Lincoln, NE	1,634	112	St. Cloud, MN	1,065
83	Santa Barbara-Santa Maria-lompoc, CA	1,597	113	Mobile, AL	1,025
83	Yolo, CA	1,597	114	Fort Collins-Loveland, CO	1,024
85	Dayton-Springfield, OH	1,591	115	Lubbock, TX	1,005
86	Columbia, SC	1,498			

3   (cont'd) INTERNATIONAL ENROLLMENTS IN MSAs WITH MORE THAN 1,000 INTERNATIONAL STUDENTS, 2001/02

State/ Region	1959/60	1969/70	1979/80	1989/90	1999/00	2000/01	2001/02	% Change from 2000/01
Alaska	0	73	185	364	392	518	479	-7.5
California	6,457	22,170	47,621	54,178	66,305	74,281	78,741	6.0
Hawaii	151	1,927	2,653	4,190	5,430	5,344	5,289	-1.0
Oregon	638	2,312	4,853	6,403	6,404	6,612	6,560	-0.8
Washington	1,031	3,238	6,717	6,858	10,965	11,370	11,624	2.2
Pacific Totals	**8,277**	**29,720**	**62,029**	**71,993**	**89,496**	**98,125**	**102,693**	**4.7**
Colorado	672	1,460	4,184	4,681	6,461	6,442	6,692	3.9
Idaho	160	500	989	1,150	1,271	1,448	1,578	9.0
Montana	162	324	401	770	1,011	998	944	-5.4
Nevada	12	109	521	783	2,450	2,755	2,927	6.2
Utah	741	1,915	3,493	4,862	5,834	6,077	5,950	-2.1
Wyoming	63	282	435	527	487	446	448	0.4
Mountain Totals	**1,810**	**4,590**	**10,023**	**12,773**	**17,514**	**18,166**	**18,539**	**2.1**
Illinois	2,890	7,795	12,218	16,816	22,807	24,229	25,498	5.2
Indiana	1,819	3,230	5,499	7,575	11,654	12,019	12,871	7.1
Iowa	776	1,285	4,010	6,735	7,218	7,840	7,896	0.7
Kansas	800	2,005	4,479	6,009	6,050	6,533	7,240	10.8
Michigan	3,259	6,774	10,559	13,555	19,151	21,120	23,103	9.4
Minnesota	1,473	2,577	4,142	5,446	7,888	8,473	8,651	2.1
Missouri	996	2,896	4,712	6,620	9,182	10,042	10,281	2.4
Nebraska	358	601	1,517	1,918	3,317	3,223	3,874	20.2
North Dakota	211	616	512	1,341	991	1,126	1,376	22.2
Ohio	1,550	4,121	8,672	13,856	16,806	18,502	19,384	4.8
South Dakota	113	262	486	758	700	745	770	3.4
Wisconsin	1,199	3,450	4,088	6,438	7,833	7,749	7,701	-0.6
Midwest Totals	**15,444**	**35,612**	**60,894**	**87,067**	**113,597**	**121,601**	**128,645**	**5.8**
Alabama	311	551	3,220	4,513	5,441	5,600	6,040	7.9
Arkansas	107	235	1,328	1,710	2,317	2,649	2,758	4.1
Delaware	38	311	447	1,003	2,016	2,091	1,975	-5.5
District of Columbia	2,020	3,949	8,499	9,487	8,202	9,094	9,241	1.6
Florida	730	6,939	11,919	20,364	24,827	25,366	28,303	11.6
Georgia	416	1,258	4,472	5,980	9,901	10,844	11,991	10.6
Kentucky	293	734	2,208	2,543	4,201	4,778	4,789	0.2
Louisiana	815	1,720	5,546	5,535	6,305	6,400	6,312	-1.4
Maryland	542	1,670	4,266	6,952	11,941	12,409	13,947	12.4
Mississippi	130	387	1,704	1,941	2,263	2,331	2,381	2.1
North Carolina	628	1,594	3,709	5,764	7,848	7,957	8,960	12.6
South Carolina	185	368	1,484	2,381	3,523	3,573	3,731	4.4
Tennessee	450	1,295	4,499	4,247	5,244	5,835	5,867	0.5
Virginia	275	662	3,374	6,970	11,616	12,782	12,600	-1.4
West Virginia	118	226	1,453	1,417	2,230	2,032	2,108	3.7
South Totals	**7,058**	**21,899**	**58,128**	**80,807**	**107,875**	**113,741**	**121,003**	**6.4**

4   INTERNATIONAL STUDENTS IN U.S. REGIONS AND STATES, SELECTED YEARS 1959/60 – 2001/02

State/Region	1959/60	1969/70	1979/80	1989/90	1999/00	2000/01	2001/02	% Change from 2000/01
Arizona	310	1,134	3,798	6,763	9,405	9,912	10,511	6.0
New Mexico	515	481	1,240	1,399	1,672	1,629	1,893	16.2
Oklahoma	717	1,554	8,464	5,989	8,041	8,263	8,818	6.7
Texas	1,574	4,902	24,416	24,170	35,860	37,735	44,192	17.1
Southwest Totals	**3,116**	**8,071**	**37,918**	**38,321**	**54,978**	**57,539**	**65,414**	**13.7**
Connecticut	573	1,314	2,847	4,636	7,110	7,358	8,050	9.4
Maine	84	262	307	902	1,282	1,256	1,357	8.0
Massachusetts	3,136	6,352	12,607	20,840	28,192	29,395	29,988	2.0
New Hampshire	102	356	501	1,262	2,068	2,301	2,436	5.9
New Jersey	583	1,738	4,767	9,608	12,179	12,558	13,516	7.6
New York	6,069	17,701	23,509	38,350	55,085	58,286	62,053	6.5
Pennsylvania	1,734	5,248	8,919	15,803	20,336	22,279	24,014	7.8
Rhode Island	191	635	949	1,858	3,176	3,375	3,370	-0.1
Vermont	136	222	702	1,206	959	949	908	-4.3
Northeast Totals	**12,608**	**33,828**	**55,108**	**94,465**	**130,387**	**137,757**	**145,692**	**5.8**
Guam	—	113	589	473	106	161	162	0.6
Puerto Rico	156	1,049	628	633	621	672	743	10.6
Virgin Islands	—	104	130	319	149	105	105	0.0
Other Totals	**156**	**1,266**	**1,347**	**1,425**	**876**	**938**	**1,010**	**7.7**
U.S. TOTAL	**48,486**	**134,959**	**286,343**	**386,851**	**514,723**	**547,867**	**582,996**	**6.4**

4 (cont'd) INTERNATIONAL STUDENTS IN U.S. REGIONS AND STATES, SELECTED YEARS 1959/60 – 2001/02

Primary Source of Funds	2000/01 Int'l Students	% of Total	2001/02 Int'l Students	% of Total	% Change
Personal & Family	366,629	66.9	395,839	67.9	8.0
U.S. College or University	108,622	19.8	120,364	20.6	10.8
Home Government/University	21,684	4.0	21,535	3.7	-0.7
U.S. Private Sponsor	13,672	2.5	15,561	2.7	13.8
Foreign Private Sponsor	13,387	2.4	11,857	2.0	-11.4
Current Employment	12,908	2.4	10,940	1.9	-15.2
Other Sources	5,108	0.9	1,369	0.2	-73.2
U.S. Government	3,553	0.6	3,677	0.6	3.5
International Organization	2,303	0.4	1,856	0.3	-19.4
Total	**547,867**	**100.0**	**582,996**	**100.0**	**6.4**

5 INTERNATIONAL STUDENTS BY PRIMARY SOURCE OF FUNDS, 2000/01 & 2001/02

Primary Source of Funds	% Under-graduate	% Graduate	% Other
Personal & Family	80.4	51.5	70.6
U.S. College or University	9.2	37.9	7
Home Government/University	3.5	3.9	3.6
U.S. Government	0.5	0.9	0.5
Private U.S. Sponsor	3.5	1.8	1.9
Foreign Private Sponsor	2.2	1.9	1.8
Current Employment	0.2	1.5	13.7
International Organization	0.2	0.5	0.5
Other Sources	0.2	0.2	0.4
Total	**100.0**	**100.0**	**100.0**

6   PRIMARY SOURCE OF FUNDING WITHIN ACADEMIC LEVEL, 2001/02

Category	1993/94	1994/95	1995/96	1996/97	1997/98	1998/99	1999/00	2000/01	2001/02	% Changes 1993-2001
TOTAL CENSUS	**449,749**	**452,635**	**453,787**	**457,984**	**481,280**	**490,933**	**514,723**	**547,867**	**582,996**	**29.6**
Research I	152,561	152,655	152,359	152,677	156,872	158,162	168,142	180,460	192,598	26.2
Research II	39,607	39,950	39,652	38,896	39,295	38,616	39,536	41,211	43,744	10.4
All Research	**192,168**	**192,605**	**192,011**	**191,573**	**196,167**	**196,778**	**207,678**	**221,671**	**236,342**	**23.0**
Doctoral I	31,836	31,599	32,464	32,835	34,573	34,700	36,714	38,495	41,278	29.7
Doctoral II	28,326	27,432	27,393	28,577	30,572	31,488	32,841	36,018	38,886	37.3
All Doctoral	**60,162**	**59,031**	**59,857**	**61,412**	**65,145**	**66,188**	**69,555**	**74,513**	**80,164**	**33.2**
Master's I	80,469	80,721	81,583	79,865	85,377	84,198	89,027	95,982	101,221	25.8
Master's II	6,923	6,667	7,058	6,575	6,928	6,662	6,922	7,694	9,106	31.5
All Master's	**87,392**	**87,388**	**88,641**	**86,440**	**92,305**	**90,860**	**95,949**	**103,676**	**110,327**	**26.2**
Baccalaureate I	8,954	8,722	9,198	8,871	9,709	9,425	10,016	9,777	10,899	21.7
Baccalaureate II	17,469	18,417	17,552	17,350	16,204	17,645	17,148	17,490	17,680	1.2
All Baccalaureate	**26,423**	**27,139**	**26,750**	**26,221**	**25,913**	**27,070**	**27,164**	**27,267**	**28,579**	**8.2**
All Associate Degree	**61,278**	**62,838**	**60,241**	**64,920**	**73,443**	**81,285**	**85,817**	**91,727**	**98,813**	**61.3**
Religious	3,342	3,034	2,992	2,741	3,185	3,329	3,346	3,212	3,156	-5.6
Medical	2,172	2,065	2,148	1,861	1,857	1,917	2,078	2,175	2,358	8.6
Other Health	1,140	1,704	1,740	2,020	1,484	2,256	1,590	1,360	1,659	45.5

7   INTERNATIONAL STUDENT ENROLLMENTS BY INSTITUTIONAL TYPE, 1993/94 – 2001/02

Category	1993/94	1994/95	1995/96	1996/97	1997/98	1998/99	1999/00	2000/01	2001/02	% Changes 1993-2001
Engineering	1,824	1,759	1,624	1,576	1,577	2,214	2,107	2,192	2,287	25.4
Business	4,958	5,867	7,685	9,020	8,885	7,358	7,798	7,838	7,673	54.8
Fine Arts	7,055	7,598	8,264	8,193	9,154	9,299	9,318	9,770	9,338	32.4
Law	12	14	23	21	93	103	345	393	332	2,666.7
Teachers	77	42	78	76	113	118	114	125	122	58.4
Other Specialized	1,733	1,532	1,720	1,895	1,948	2,147	1,864	1,944	1,838	6.1
Tribal Colleges	14	17	13	15	11	11	0	4	8	-42.9
All Specialized	**22,327**	**23,632**	**26,287**	**27,418**	**28,307**	**28,752**	**28,560**	**29,013**	**28,771**	**28.9**

7   (cont'd) **INTERNATIONAL STUDENT ENROLLMENTS BY INSTITUTIONAL TYPE, 1993/94 – 2001/02**

8 ENROLLMENT OF 20 LEADING NATIONALITIES BY INSTITUTIONAL TYPE, 2001/02

RANK	RESEARCH I&II Country	% of Enrollment	DOCTORAL I&II Country	% of Enrollment	MASTER'S I&II Country	% of Enrollment	BACCALAUREATE I&II Country	% of Enrollment	ASSOCIATE Country	% of Enrollment	OTHER INSTITUTIONS Country	% of Enrollment
1	China	15.6	India	16.9	India	11.0	Japan	10.6	Japan	17.7	Korea, Rep. of	15.4
2	India	13.5	China	11.4	Japan	9.9	Canada	8.9	Korea, Rep. of	7.5	Japan	8.4
3	Korea, Rep. of	10.2	Korea, Rep. of	5.6	China	6.8	Korea, Rep. of	5.4	Taiwan	3.7	Canada	7.8
4	Japan	5.1	Japan	5.5	Taiwan	6.2	India	5.3	Mexico	3.7	India	7.1
5	Taiwan	5.1	Taiwan	4.5	Korea, Rep. of	5.5	China	3.2	China	3.6	China	6.5
6	Canada	4.6	Canada	3.3	Canada	5.1	Taiwan	2.8	Indonesia	3.3	Taiwan	5.9
7	Turkey	2.4	Thailand	2.6	Mexico	3.4	Kenya	2.3	Hong Kong	2.8	Thailand	2.2
8	Indonesia	1.9	Turkey	2.0	Thailand	2.5	United Kingdom	2.3	India	2.7	Turkey	1.9
9	Thailand	1.9	Pakistan	1.8	Indonesia	2.1	Pakistan	2.1	Colombia	2.6	Indonesia	1.9
10	Germany	1.9	France	1.6	Turkey	2.1	Brazil	2.0	Brazil	2.3	Germany	1.7
11	Mexico	1.7	Colombia	1.5	Kenya	2.1	Bulgaria	1.9	Kenya	2.3	Brazil	1.7
12	United Kingdom	1.6	Germany	1.5	Pakistan	1.9	Ghana	1.8	Canada	2.1	Kenya	1.6
13	France	1.5	Saudi Arabia	1.5	Germany	1.6	Germany	1.6	Jamaica	1.8	Sweden	1.4
14	Brazil	1.5	Malaysia	1.4	Malaysia	1.4	Jamaica	1.6	Pakistan	1.8	Pakistan	1.3
15	Malaysia	1.4	Brazil	1.3	United Kingdom	1.3	Russia	1.5	Venezuela	1.6	United Kingdom	1.3
16	Hong Kong	1.3	Indonesia	1.3	Colombia	1.3	Nepal	1.5	Turkey	1.5	Malaysia	1.2
17	Pakistan	1.2	United Kingdom	1.3	Brazil	1.3	Bahamas	1.3	Vietnam	1.5	Colombia	1.2
18	Singapore	1.2	Mexico	1.2	Nigeria	1.2	Turkey	1.3	Thailand	1.3	Mexico	1.2
19	Russia	1.2	Venezuela	1.2	Russia	1.1	France	1.3	Germany	1.3	Israel	1.2
20	Colombia	1.1	Jamaica	1.2	Hong Kong	1.1	Mexico	1.3	Russia	1.3	Philippines	1.1
TOTAL	236,342		80,164		110,327		28,579		98,813		28,771	

Rank	Institution	City	State	Total Int'l Students	Total Enrollment
1	University of Southern California	Los Angeles	CA	5,950	29,813
2	New York University	New York	NY	5,504	37,134
3	Columbia University	New York	NY	5,116	22,425
4	Purdue University Main Campus	West Lafayette	IN	4,695	37,871
5	University of Texas at Austin	Austin	TX	4,673	50,616
6	Boston University	Boston	MA	4,412	27,767
7	The Ohio State University Main Campus	Columbus	OH	4,302	48,477
8	University of Illinois at Urbana-Champaign	Champaign	IL	4,287	37,684
9	University of Michigan – Ann Arbor	Ann Arbor	MI	4,149	38,248
10	University of Florida	Gainesville	FL	3,884	45,937
11	University of Pennsylvania	Philadelphia	PA	3,820	21,853
12	University of Wisconsin – Madison	Madison	WI	3,744	41,552
13	University of Maryland College Park	College Park	MD	3,711	34,160
14	Texas A&M University	College Station	TX	3,563	44,689
15	Penn State University Park	University Park	PA	3,484	40,828
16	Harvard University	Cambridge	MA	3,448	18,308
17	University of Houston	Houston	TX	3,380	33,007
18	University of Minnesota – Twin Cities	Minneapolis	MN	3,356	47,597
19	Arizona State University Main	Tempe	AZ	3,348	45,693
20	Indiana University at Bloomington	Bloomington	IN	3,325	37,963
21	SUNY at Buffalo	Buffalo	NY	3,237	25,838
22	Wayne State University	Detroit	MI	3,233	31,040
23	Cornell University	Ithaca	NY	3,181	19,420
24	Michigan State University	East Lansing	MI	3,021	44,227
25	University of Arizona	Tucson	AZ	2,951	32,870
26	Stanford University	Stanford	CA	2,922	14,248
27	University of Illinois at Chicago	Chicago	IL	2,898	24,530
28	University of California – Los Angeles	Los Angeles	CA	2,794	36,890
29	Rutgers University – New Brunswick Campus	New Brunswick	NJ	2,779	35,308
30	University of Washington	Seattle	WA	2,736	37,412
31	University of California – Berkeley	Berkeley	CA	2,735	32,128
32	Massachusetts Institute of Technology	Cambridge	MA	2,734	10,698
33	Northeastern University	Boston	MA	2,729	24,706
34	University of South Florida	Tampa	FL	2,573	37,814
35	Georgia Institute of Technology	Atlanta	GA	2,547	15,401
36	Iowa State University	Ames	IA	2,455	27,644
37	Carnegie Mellon University	Pittsburgh	PA	2,395	8,588
38	University of Chicago	Chicago	IL	2,173	12,705
39	Syracuse University	Syracuse	NY	2,132	18,105
40	Virginia Polytechnic Institute & State University	Blacksburg	VA	2,087	25,000

9   INTERNATIONAL STUDENTS BY INSTITUTIONAL TYPE: TOP 40 RESEARCH INSTITUTIONS, 2001/02

Rank	Institution	City	State	Total Int'l Students	Total Enrollment
1	Florida International University	Miami	FL	3,723	31,822
2	University of Texas at Arlington	Arlington	TX	2,310	21,273
3	University of North Texas	Denton	TX	2,102	28,150
4	Western Michigan University	Kalamazoo	MI	2,010	28,931
5	George Mason University	Fairfax	VA	1,888	24,900
6	Illinois Institute of Technology	Chicago	IL	1,869	6,050
7	University of Texas at Dallas	Richardson	TX	1,858	12,605
8	New School University	New York	NY	1,740	7,764
9	Georgia State University	Atlanta	GA	1,677	25,235
10	American University	Washington	DC	1,582	11,421
11	Drexel University	Philadelphia	PA	1,581	11,641
12	New Jersey Institute of Technology	Newark	NJ	1,553	8,862
13	Wichita State University	Wichita	KS	1,493	14,854
14	Florida Atlantic University	Boca Raton	FL	1,469	23,537
15	Old Dominion University	Norfolk	VA	1,366	19,627
16	San Diego State University	San Diego	CA	1,331	33,285
17	University of Toledo	Toledo	OH	1,251	20,313
18	DePaul University	Chicago	IL	1,049	20,548
19	Binghamton University – SUNY	Binghamton	NY	1,028	12,820
20	Portland State University	Portland	OR	1,026	20,185
21	University of Nevada, Reno	Reno	NV	957	14,000
22	Pace University	New York	NY	941	8,150
23	University of Missouri – Kansas City	Kansas City	MO	924	12,969
24	University of Denver	Denver	CO	920	9,271
25	Florida Institute of Technology	Melbourne	FL	902	4,409
26	University of Central Florida	Orlando	FL	894	35,927
27	University of Alabama	Tuscaloosa	AL	885	19,171
28	Indiana U. – Purdue U. Indianapolis	Indianapolis	IN	873	27,525
29	University of Colorado at Denver	Denver	CO	861	11,050
30	University of Maryland Baltimore County	Baltimore	MD	860	11,237
31	CUNY Graduate Center	New York	NY	856	3,872
32	Boston College	Chestnut Hill	MA	852	14,419
33	Rutgers University – Newark Campus	Newark	NJ	849	9,602
34	Saint John's University	Jamaica	NY	827	18,623
35	Cleveland State University	Cleveland	OH	826	826
36	The University of Akron, Main Campus	Akron	OH	824	24,358
37	Southern Methodist University	Dallas	TX	781	10,266
38	University of Massachusetts Lowell	Lowell	MA	780	12,397
39	University of New Orleans	New Orleans	LA	766	17,014
40	University of Missouri – Rolla	Rolla	MO	732	4,748

10   INTERNATIONAL STUDENTS BY INSTITUTIONAL TYPE: TOP 40 DOCTORAL INSTITUTIONS, 2001/02

Rank	Institution	City	State	Total Int'l Students	Total Enrollment
1	CUNY Baruch College	New York	NY	3,043	15,423
2	San Francisco State University	San Francisco	CA	2,566	26,804
3	California State University – Long Beach	Long Beach	CA	2,266	33,259
4	University of Texas at El Paso	El Paso	TX	2,054	16,220
5	Hawaii Pacific University	Honolulu	HI	1,851	8,033
6	University of Bridgeport	Bridgeport	CT	1,594	3,313
7	University of Central Oklahoma	Edmond	OK	1,522	14,564
8	California State University – Hayward	Hayward	CA	1,480	13,487
9	CUNY City College	New York	NY	1,475	11,136
10	San Jose State University	San Jose	CA	1,471	27,000
11	Rochester Institute of Technology	Rochester	NY	1,433	15,160
12	California State University – Fullerton	Fullerton	CA	1,350	29,000
13	Eastern Michigan University	Ypsilanti	MI	1,304	24,287
14	California State University – Northridge	Northridge	CA	1,264	29,066
15	Strayer College	Washington	DC	1,204	14,009
16	University of Nevada – Las Vegas	Las Vegas	NV	1,198	23,618
17	D'Youville College	Buffalo	NY	1,122	2,486
18	NY Instit. of Tech. Main Campus – Old Westbury	Old Westbury	NY	1,016	9,456
18	Oklahoma City University	Oklahoma City	OK	1,016	3,705
18	California State Polytechnic University – Pomona	Pomona	CA	1,016	19,041
21	Fairleigh Dickinson University	Teaneck	NJ	960	9,684
22	University of North Carolina at Charlotte	Charlotte	NC	958	18,000
23	CUNY Brooklyn College	Brooklyn	NY	951	15,039
24	Saint Cloud State University	St. Cloud	MN	918	15,181
25	University of Massachusetts Boston	Boston	MA	873	12,000
26	University of South Alabama	Mobile	AL	868	11,673
27	Golden Gate University	San Francisco	CA	831	4,810
28	California State University – Los Angeles	Los Angeles	CA	817	19,593
29	Montclair State University	Upper Montclair	NJ	814	13,855
30	California State University – Fresno	Fresno	CA	768	20,013
31	University of Nebraska at Omaha	Omaha	NE	760	15,106
32	Towson University	Towson	MD	740	16,729
33	CUNY Hunter College	New York	NY	738	20,149
34	California State University – Sacramento	Sacramento	CA	724	26,924
35	California State University – San Bernardino	San Bernardino	CA	695	695
36	Santa Clara University	Santa Clara	CA	693	7,592
37	Suffolk University	Boston	MA	685	5,314
38	Embry-Riddle Aeronautical University	Daytona Beach	FL	669	4,803
39	University of Texas – Pan American	Edinburg	TX	661	13,640
40	University of Houston – Clear Lake	Houston	TX	616	7,738

11 INTERNATIONAL STUDENTS BY INSTITUTIONAL TYPE: TOP 40 MASTER'S INSTITUTIONS, 2001/02

Rank	Institution	City	State	Total Int'l Students	Total Enrollment
1	Brigham Young University Hawaii Campus	Laie Oahu	HI	942	2,278
2	Columbia College	Chicago	IL	642	9,056
3	University of Findlay	Findlay	OH	427	4,586
4	University of Dallas	Irving	TX	402	3,575
5	Mount Holyoke College	South Hadley	MA	390	2,023
6	Penn State U. – The Commonwealth College	University Park	PA	363	24,000
7	University of Houston – Downtown	Houston	TX	351	8,951
8	Lock Haven University of Pennsylvania	Lock Haven	PA	338	4,125
9	University of Hawaii at Hilo	Hilo	HI	298	2,800
10	Metropolitan State College of Denver	Denver	CO	275	17,504
11	Daemen College	Amherst	NY	266	1,984
12	Ramapo College of New Jersey	Mahwah	NJ	257	5,195
13	Macalester College	St. Paul	MN	249	1,787
14	University of Maine at Fort Kent	Fort Kent	ME	248	892
15	Saint Mary's College of Ave Maria University	Orchard Lake	MI	229	500
16	Ohio Wesleyan University	Delaware	OH	227	1,844
17	Mercy College	Dobbs Ferry	NY	225	9,932
18	Eckerd College	St. Petersburg	FL	221	1,488
19	CUNY York College	Jamaica	NY	220	5,392
20	University of Southern Colorado	Pueblo	CO	211	4,089
21	North Park University	Chicago	IL	205	2,665
22	Oberlin College	Oberlin	OH	199	2,840
23	Oakwood College	Huntsville	AL	189	1,778
24	Smith College	Northampton	MA	187	2,901
24	Metropolitan State University	St. Paul	MN	187	5,623
26	Willamette University	Salem	OR	182	2,434
27	Hamline University	St. Paul	MN	179	3,200
28	Teikyo Loretto Heights University	Denver	CO	177	181
29	Drew University	Madison	NJ	176	2,418
30	Wesleyan University	Middletown	CT	175	3,210
31	Marymount Manhattan College	New York	NY	174	2,680
31	Purchase College, SUNY	Purchase	NY	174	4,018
33	Middlebury College	Middlebury	VT	171	2,270
34	Southwestern Adventist University	Keene	TX	167	1,191
35	Morehouse College	Atlanta	GA	166	2,970
36	Wellesley College	Wellesley	MA	164	2,273
37	Bryn Mawr College	Bryn Mawr	PA	161	1,756
37	Luther College	Decorah	IA	161	2,575
39	Lewis & Clark College	Portland	OR	157	3,042
40	Concordia College – Moorhead	Moorhead	MN	154	2,766

12 INTERNATIONAL STUDENTS BY INSTITUTIONAL TYPE: TOP 40 BACCALAUREATE INSTITUTIONS, 2001/02

Rank	Institution	City	State	Total Int'l Students	Total Enrollment
1	Houston Community College System	Houston	TX	3,484	40,929
2	Montgomery College	Rockville	MD	3,217	22,793
3	Santa Monica College	Santa Monica	CA	3,074	27,991
4	Northern Virginia Community College	Annandale	VA	2,267	39,138
5	De Anza College	Cupertino	CA	2,242	28,000
6	CUNY Borough of Manhattan Community College	New York	NY	1,692	15,875
7	Miami-Dade Community College	Miami	FL	1,592	23,958
8	Seminole Community College	Sanford	FL	1,577	7,993
9	Foothill College	Los Altos Hills	CA	1,573	26,754
10	City College of San Francisco	San Francisco	CA	1,445	66,686
11	CUNY La Guardia Community College	Long Island City	NY	1,232	11,599
12	Pasadena City College	Pasadena	CA	1,201	28,000
13	Broward Community College	Fort Lauderdale	FL	1,200	25,438
14	Orange Coast College	Costa Mesa	CA	1,152	24,480
15	Diablo Valley College	Pleasant Hill	CA	982	24,000
16	Nassau Community College	Garden City	NY	960	19,712
17	Collin County Community College District	Plano	TX	880	14,497
18	El Camino College	Torrance	CA	875	24,000
19	CUNY Queensborough Community College	Bayside	NY	869	11,109
20	Austin Community College	Austin	TX	868	25,735
21	Oakland Community College	Farmington Hills	MI	829	24,360
22	Los Angeles City College	Los Angeles	CA	800	22,137
23	North Lake College	Irving	TX	791	8,217
24	Moraine Valley Community College	Palos Hills	IL	785	14,033
25	Bellevue Community College	Bellevue	WA	778	21,772
26	Georgia Perimeter College	Clarkston	GA	762	15,372
27	Seattle Central Community College	Seattle	WA	740	10,697
28	Grossmont College	El Cajon	CA	710	16,911
29	Pima County Community College District	Tucson	AZ	676	28,466
30	Edmonds Community College	Lynnwood	WA	648	11,206
31	El Paso Community College	El Paso	TX	634	17,901
32	Rancho Santiago C.C. District/Santa Ana College	Santa Ana	CA	627	39,599
33	Glendale Community College	Glendale	CA	611	15,000
34	Norwalk Community College	Norwalk	CT	600	5,377
34	North Harris Montgomery Community C. District	Houston	TX	600	22,113
36	Quincy College	Quincy	MA	554	5,290
37	Butler County Community College	El Dorado	KS	552	7,911
38	Washtenaw Community College	Ann Arbor	MI	543	11,089
39	East Los Angeles College	Monterey Park	CA	529	20,362
40	St. Petersburg College	St. Petersburg	FL	527	60,697

13   INTERNATIONAL STUDENTS BY INSTITUTIONAL TYPE: TOP 40 ASSOCIATE INSTITUTIONS, 2001/02

Rank	Institution	City	State	Total Int'l Students	Total Enrollment
1	Academy of Art College	San Francisco	CA	1,752	6,019
2	Johnson & Wales University	Providence	RI	1,161	13,932
3	Fashion Institute of Technology	New York	NY	1,148	7,493
4	Berklee College of Music	Boston	MA	1,030	3,415
5	Pratt Institute	Brooklyn	NY	821	4,358
6	Southern New Hampshire University	Manchester	NH	742	5,500
7	Thunderbird, The Amer. Grad. Sch. of Int'l Mgmt.	Glendale	AZ	724	1,142
8	Babson College	Babson Park	MA	614	3,328
9	School of Visual Arts	New York	NY	600	5,485
10	Southern Polytechnic State University	Marietta	GA	565	3,543
11	Bentley College	Waltham	MA	561	5,728
12	Franklin University	Columbus	OH	555	5,537
13	Life University	Marietta	GA	532	3,158
14	Savannah College of Art and Design	Savannah	GA	519	4,923
15	Northwood University	Midland	MI	448	5,818
16	Fuller Theological Seminary	Pasadena	CA	415	2,859
17	Lynn University	Boca Raton	FL	410	1,557
18	Southeastern University	Washington	DC	351	982
19	Art Center College of Design	Pasadena	CA	332	1,462
20	University of Baltimore	Baltimore	MD	312	4,674
21	School of the Art Institute of Chicago	Chicago	IL	309	2,115
22	Monterey Institute of International Studies	Monterey	CA	302	683
23	Rhode Island School of Design	Providence	RI	278	2,119
24	U. of Texas Health Science Center at Houston	Houston	TX	269	3,286
25	Naval Postgraduate School	Monterey	CA	264	1,297
26	Manhattan School of Music	New York	NY	263	765
27	Southwestern Baptist Theological Seminary	Fort Worth	TX	249	2,839
28	Goldey-Beacom College	Wilmington	DE	246	1,500
28	New England Conservatory of Music	Boston	MA	246	732
30	University of Maryland Baltimore	Baltimore	MD	245	5,337
31	Johns Hopkins University SAIS	Washington	DC	231	515
32	The Juilliard School	New York	NY	218	813
33	University of Tennessee Health Science Center	Memphis	TN	209	2,015
34	Palmer College of Chiropractic	Davenport	IA	208	1,670
35	Wentworth Institute of Technology	Boston	MA	200	2,731
35	Tufts U. – Fletcher School of Law & Diplomacy	Medford	MA	200	9,167
37	South Dakota School of Mines and Technology	Rapid City	SD	198	2,424
38	Bryant College	Smithfield	RI	191	3,494
39	Peabody Institute of Johns Hopkins University	Baltimore	MD	188	680
40	Kettering University	Flint	MI	183	3,346

14 INTERNATIONAL STUDENTS BY INSTITUTIONAL TYPE: TOP 40 PROFESSIONAL & SPECIALIZED INSTITUTIONS, 2001/02

Rank	Institution	City	State	Total Int'l Students	Total Enrollment
1	University of Southern California	Los Angeles	CA	5,950	29,813
2	New York University	New York	NY	5,504	37,134
3	Columbia University	New York	NY	5,116	22,425
4	Purdue University Main Campus	West Lafayette	IN	4,695	37,871
5	University of Texas at Austin	Austin	TX	4,673	50,616
6	Boston University	Boston	MA	4,412	27,767
7	The Ohio State University Main Campus	Columbus	OH	4,302	48,477
8	University of Illinois at Urbana-Champaign	Champaign	IL	4,287	37,684
9	University of Michigan – Ann Arbor	Ann Arbor	MI	4,149	38,248
10	University of Florida	Gainesville	FL	3,884	45,937
11	University of Pennsylvania	Philadelphia	PA	3,820	21,853
12	University of Wisconsin – Madison	Madison	WI	3,744	41,552
13	Florida International University	Miami	FL	3,723	31,822
14	University of Maryland College Park	College Park	MD	3,711	34,160
15	Texas A&M University	College Station	TX	3,563	44,689
16	Penn State University Park	University Park	PA	3,484	40,828
16	Houston Community College System	Houston	TX	3,484	40,929
18	Harvard University	Cambridge	MA	3,448	18,308
19	University of Houston	Houston	TX	3,380	33,007
20	University of Minnesota – Twin Cities	Minneapolis	MN	3,356	47,597
21	Arizona State University Main	Tempe	AZ	3,348	45,693
22	Indiana University at Bloomington	Bloomington	IN	3,325	37,963
23	SUNY at Buffalo	Buffalo	NY	3,237	25,838
24	Wayne State University	Detroit	MI	3,233	31,040
25	Montgomery College	Rockville	MD	3,217	22,793
26	Cornell University	Ithaca	NY	3,181	19,420
27	Santa Monica College	Santa Monica	CA	3,074	27,991
28	CUNY Baruch College	New York	NY	3,043	15,423
29	Michigan State University	East Lansing	MI	3,021	44,227
30	University of Arizona	Tucson	AZ	2,951	32,870
31	Stanford University	Stanford	CA	2,922	14,248
32	University of Illinois at Chicago	Chicago	IL	2,898	24,530
33	University of California – Los Angeles	Los Angeles	CA	2,794	36,890
34	Rutgers University – New Brunswick Campus	New Brunswick	NJ	2,779	35,308
35	University of Washington	Seattle	WA	2,736	37,412
36	University of California – Berkeley	Berkeley	CA	2,735	32,128
37	Massachusetts Institute of Technology	Cambridge	MA	2,734	10,698
38	Northeastern University	Boston	MA	2,729	24,706
39	University of South Florida	Tampa	FL	2,573	37,814
40	San Francisco State University	San Francisco	CA	2,566	26,804
41	Georgia Institute of Technology	Atlanta	GA	2,547	15,401
42	Iowa State University	Ames	IA	2,455	27,644
43	Carnegie Mellon University	Pittsburgh	PA	2,395	8,588
44	University of Texas at Arlington	Arlington	TX	2,310	21,273
45	Northern Virginia Community College	Annandale	VA	2,267	39,138

15 INSTITUTIONS WITH 1,000 OR MORE INTERNATIONAL STUDENTS, 2001/02 RANKED BY INTERNATIONAL STUDENT TOTALS

Rank	Institution	City	State	Total Int'l Students	Total Enrollment
46	California State University – Long Beach	Long Beach	CA	2,266	33,259
47	De Anza College	Cupertino	CA	2,242	28,000
48	University of Chicago	Chicago	IL	2,173	12,705
49	Syracuse University	Syracuse	NY	2,132	18,105
50	University of North Texas	Denton	TX	2,102	28,150
51	Virginia Polytechnic Institute & State University	Blacksburg	VA	2,087	25,000
52	George Washington University	Washington	DC	2,072	22,184
53	University of Texas at El Paso	El Paso	TX	2,054	16,220
54	University of Iowa	Iowa City	IA	2,027	28,768
55	Western Michigan University	Kalamazoo	MI	2,010	28,931
56	Oklahoma State University Main Campus	Stillwater	OK	1,995	21,872
57	Yale University	New Haven	CT	1,967	11,126
58	Brigham Young University	Provo	UT	1,926	32,771
59	University of Miami	Coral Gables	FL	1,919	14,436
60	Temple University	Philadelphia	PA	1,894	29,946
61	George Mason University	Fairfax	VA	1,888	24,900
62	SUNY at Stony Brook	Stony Brook	NY	1,876	20,855
63	Illinois Institute of Technology	Chicago	IL	1,869	6,050
64	University of Texas at Dallas	Richardson	TX	1,858	12,605
65	Hawaii Pacific University	Honolulu	HI	1,851	8,033
66	North Carolina State University	Raleigh	NC	1,844	28,619
67	University of Cincinnati	Cincinnati	OH	1,827	33,187
68	University of Massachusetts	Amherst	MA	1,823	23,600
69	Southern Illinois University Carbondale	Carbondale	IL	1,768	20,933
70	University of Oregon	Eugene	OR	1,766	19,091
71	Northwestern University	Evanston	IL	1,765	15,201
72	Academy of Art College	San Francisco	CA	1,752	6,019
73	New School University	New York	NY	1,740	7,764
74	Louisiana State University and A & M College	Baton Rouge	LA	1,721	31,402
75	CUNY Borough of Manhattan Community College	New York	NY	1,692	15,875
76	University of Pittsburgh, Pittsburgh Campus	Pittsburgh	PA	1,682	26,710
77	University of Kansas Main Campus	Lawrence	KS	1,677	26,000
77	Georgia State University	Atlanta	GA	1,677	25,235
79	University of California – San Diego	La Jolla	CA	1,675	21,568
80	Duke University	Durham	NC	1,640	12,555
81	University of Oklahoma Norman Campus	Norman	OK	1,601	24,890
82	University of California – Davis	Davis	CA	1,597	26,513
82	University of California – Irvine	Irvine	CA	1,597	21,338
84	University of Bridgeport	Bridgeport	CT	1,594	3,313
85	Miami-Dade Community College	Miami	FL	1,592	23,958
86	University of Utah	Salt Lake City	UT	1,584	26,182
87	American University	Washington	DC	1,582	11,421
88	Drexel University	Philadelphia	PA	1,581	11,641
89	Seminole Community College	Sanford	FL	1,577	7,993

15 (cont'd) INSTITUTIONS WITH 1,000 OR MORE INTERNATIONAL STUDENTS, 2001/02
RANKED BY INTERNATIONAL STUDENT TOTALS

Rank	Institution	City	State	Total Int'l Students	Total Enrollment
90	Foothill College	Los Altos Hills	CA	1,573	26,754
91	University of Connecticut	Storrs	CT	1,555	23,419
92	New Jersey Institute of Technology	Newark	NJ	1,553	8,862
93	University of Central Oklahoma	Edmond	OK	1,522	14,564
94	Wichita State University	Wichita	KS	1,493	14,854
95	California State University – Hayward	Hayward	CA	1,480	13,487
96	CUNY City College	New York	NY	1,475	11,136
97	San Jose State University	San Jose	CA	1,471	27,000
97	University of Hawaii at Manoa	Honolulu	HI	1,471	17,532
99	Florida Atlantic University	Boca Raton	FL	1,469	23,537
100	University of Nebraska – Lincoln	Lincoln	NE	1,462	22,764
101	Georgetown University	Washington	DC	1,454	12,500
102	City College of San Francisco	San Francisco	CA	1,445	66,686
103	Rochester Institute of Technology	Rochester	NY	1,433	15,160
104	University of Georgia	Athens	GA	1,432	32,317
105	University of Kentucky	Lexington	KY	1,421	23,114
106	University of Virginia	Charlottesville	VA	1,400	22,411
107	University of Delaware	Newark	DE	1,384	20,949
108	University of Missouri – Columbia	Columbia	MO	1,371	23,666
109	Old Dominion University	Norfolk	VA	1,366	19,627
110	California State University – Fullerton	Fullerton	CA	1,350	29,000
111	University of North Carolina at Chapel Hill	Chapel Hill	NC	1,347	25,480
112	San Diego State University	San Diego	CA	1,331	33,285
113	University of Rochester	Rochester	NY	1,326	8,351
114	Washington University	St. Louis	MO	1,325	12,187
115	Eastern Michigan University	Ypsilanti	MI	1,304	24,287
116	California State University – Northridge	Northridge	CA	1,264	29,066
117	Case Western Reserve University	Cleveland	OH	1,251	9,216
117	University of Toledo	Toledo	OH	1,251	20,313
119	CUNY La Guardia Community College	Long Island City	NY	1,232	11,599
120	Howard University	Washington	DC	1,223	10,700
121	Oregon State University	Corvallis	OR	1,217	18,034
122	University of South Carolina – Columbia	Columbia	SC	1,214	23,000
123	West Virginia University	Morgantown	WV	1,207	22,774
124	Strayer College	Washington	DC	1,204	14,009
125	Pasadena City College	Pasadena	CA	1,201	28,000
126	Broward Community College	Fort Lauderdale	FL	1,200	25,438
127	University of Nevada – Las Vegas	Las Vegas	NV	1,198	23,618
128	Washington State University	Pullman	WA	1,178	20,492
129	Ohio University Main Campus	Athens	OH	1,168	19,661
129	Kansas State University	Manhattan	KS	1,168	22,396
131	Johnson & Wales University	Providence	RI	1,161	13,932
132	Orange Coast College	Costa Mesa	CA	1,152	24,480
133	Fashion Institute of Technology	New York	NY	1,148	7,493
134	Princeton University	Princeton	NJ	1,144	6,537

15 (cont'd) INSTITUTIONS WITH 1,000 OR MORE INTERNATIONAL STUDENTS, 2001/02
RANKED BY INTERNATIONAL STUDENT TOTALS

Rank	Institution	City	State	Total Int'l Students	Total Enrollment
135	Rensselaer Polytechnic Institute	Troy	NY	1,143	7,275
136	Brown University	Providence	RI	1,135	7,309
137	D'Youville College	Buffalo	NY	1,122	2,486
138	University of Colorado at Boulder	Boulder	CO	1,108	26,597
139	Johns Hopkins University	Baltimore	MD	1,092	17,967
140	Florida State University	Tallahassee	FL	1,052	35,462
140	Vanderbilt University	Nashville	TN	1,052	10,496
142	DePaul University	Chicago	IL	1,049	20,548
143	Berklee College of Music	Boston	MA	1,030	3,415
144	Binghamton University – SUNY	Binghamton	NY	1,028	12,820
145	Portland State University	Portland	OR	1,026	20,185
146	Colorado State University	Fort Collins	CO	1,024	23,934
147	Mississippi State University	Mississippi State	MS	1,022	16,561
148	NY Instit. of Tech. Main Campus – Old Westbury	Old Westbury	NY	1,016	9,456
148	Oklahoma City University	Oklahoma City	OK	1,016	3,705
148	California State Polytechnic University – Pomona	Pomona	CA	1,016	19,041

15 (cont'd) INSTITUTIONS WITH 1,000 OR MORE INTERNATIONAL STUDENTS, 2001/02
RANKED BY INTERNATIONAL STUDENT TOTALS

Field of Study	2000/01 Int'l Students	2001/02 Int'l Students	% of Total	% Change
Agriculture, Total	**7,200**	**7,950**	**1.4**	**10.4**
Agricultural Sciences	3,259	3,651	0.6	12.0
Conservation & Renewable Natural Resources	1,827	2,034	0.3	11.3
Business & Management, Total	**106,043**	**114,885**	**19.7**	**8.3**
Business & Management, General	100,146	108,281	18.6	8.1
Marketing & Distribution	5,068	5,214	0.9	2.9
Consumer, Personal, & Miscellaneous Services	829	1,390	0.2	67.7
Education	**14,053**	**15,709**	**2.7**	**11.8**
Engineering, Total	**83,186**	**88,181**	**15.1**	**6.0**
Engineering, General	75,815	79,833	13.7	5.3
Engineering-Related Technologies	5,630	5,655	1.0	0.4
Transportation & Material Moving	674	1,428	0.2	111.9
Mechanics & Repairers	497	660	0.1	32.8
Construction Trades	371	437	0.1	17.8
Precision Production	199	168	0.0	-15.6

16 INTERNATIONAL STUDENTS BY FIELD OF STUDY, 2000/01 & 2001/02

Field of Study	2000/01 Int'l Students	2001/02 Int'l Students	% of Total	% Change
Fine & Applied Arts, Total	**34,220**	**33,978**	**5.8**	**-0.7**
Visual & Performing Arts	27,618	27,284	4.7	-1.2
Architecture & Environmental Design	6,602	6,694	1.1	1.4
Health Professions	**22,430**	**24,037**	**4.1**	**7.2**
Humanities, Total	**16,123**	**18,367**	**3.2**	**13.9**
Letters	5,735	5,795	1.0	1.0
Foreign Languages	4,889	6,097	1.0	24.7
Theology	3,714	3,845	0.7	3.5
Philosophy & Religion	1,785	2,630	0.5	47.3
Mathematics & Computer Sciences, Total	**67,825**	**76,736**	**13.2**	**13.1**
Computer & Information Sciences	59,836	67,850	11.6	13.4
Mathematics	7,989	8,886	1.5	11.2
Physical & Life Sciences, Total	**38,396**	**41,417**	**7.1**	**7.9**
Physical Sciences	16,975	19,433	3.3	14.5
Life Sciences	20,119	20,672	3.5	2.7
Science Technologies	1,302	1,312	0.2	0.8
Social Sciences, Total	**42,367**	**44,667**	**7.7**	**5.4**
Social Sciences, General	24,057	26,208	4.5	8.9
Psychology	7,855	7,729	1.3	-1.6
Public Affairs	4,626	4,884	0.8	5.6
Area & Ethnic Studies	2,402	2,420	0.4	0.7
Protective Services	697	749	0.1	7.5
Parks & Recreation	2,730	2,677	0.5	-1.9
Other, Total	**57,235**	**59,785**	**10.3**	**4.5**
Liberal/General Studies	28,957	29,950	5.1	3.4
Communications	9,958	10,560	1.8	6.0
Law	5,759	6,552	1.1	13.8
Multi/Interdisciplinary Studies	6,388	6,840	1.2	7.1
Home Economics	2,375	2,318	0.4	-2.4
Library & Archival Sciences	816	803	0.1	-1.6
Vocational Home Economics	511	650	0.1	27.2
Communication Technologies	2,261	2,035	0.3	-10.0
Military Technologies	210	77	0.0	-63.3
Intensive English Language	**23,011**	**21,237**	**3.6**	**-7.7**
Undeclared	**35,779**	**36,048**	**6.2**	**0.8**
TOTAL	**547,867**	**582,996**		**6.4**

16 (cont'd) INTERNATIONAL STUDENTS BY FIELD OF STUDY, 2000/01 & 2001/02

Research Institutions	% Enrollment
Engineering	22.3
Business & Management	14.9
Physical & Life Sciences	10.6
Mathematics & Computer Sciences	9.8
Social Sciences	9.6
Other	9.0
Fine & Applied Arts	4.5
Health Professions	4.3
Undeclared	4.1
Humanities	3.0
Intensive English	3.0
Agriculture	2.5
Education	2.3

Doctoral Institutions	% Enrollment
Business & Management	21.4
Engineering	17.8
Mathematics & Computer Sciences	17.1
Social Sciences	7.3
Physical & Life Sciences	6.7
Other	6.5
Undeclared	6.0
Fine & Applied Arts	4.9
Intensive English	3.5
Health Professions	3.0
Humanities	2.9
Education	2.2
Agriculture	0.7

Master's Institutions	% Enrollment
Business & Management	29.5
Mathematics & Computer Sciences	18.3
Engineering	9.3
Other	8.1
Social Sciences	6.4
Undeclared	5.5
Intensive English	5.1
Education	4.1
Physical & Life Sciences	4.1
Fine & Applied Arts	3.8
Health Professions	2.8
Humanities	2.3
Agriculture	0.6

Baccalaureate Institutions	% Enrollment
Business & Management	20.9
Undeclared	16.6
Social Sciences	13.0
Mathematics & Computer Sciences	10.7
Other	9.7
Physical & Life Sciences	5.9
Humanities	5.6
Education	4.7
Fine & Applied Arts	4.4
Intensive English	3.3
Engineering	2.9
Health Professions	1.7
Agriculture	0.6

Associate Degree Institutions	% Enrollment
Other	24.2
Business & Management	19.0
Mathematics & Computer Sciences	15.8
Undeclared	12.4
Intensive English	5.3
Engineering	5.0
Health Professions	4.5
Fine & Applied Arts	4.3
Social Sciences	2.7
Education	2.5
Physical & Life Sciences	2.1
Humanities	1.6
Agriculture	0.4

Other Specialized Institutions	% Enrollment
Fine & Applied Arts	31.5
Business & Management	21.4
Health Professions	11.7
Humanities	9.2
Mathematics & Computer Sciences	7.2
Engineering	4.8
Social Sciences	4.2
Other	4.0
Physical & Life Sciences	3.1
Undeclared	1.3
Education	0.8
Intensive English	0.7
Agriculture	0.0

17   FIELDS OF STUDY BY INSTITUTIONAL TYPE, 2001/02

Academic Level	Int'l Students	2000/01 % of Total	Int'l Students	2001/02 % of Total	% Change
Associate	**67,493**	**12.3**	**67,667**	**11.6**	**0.3**
Bachelor's	**186,936**	**34.1**	**193,412**	**33.2**	**3.5**
Freshman	38,167	7.0	38,693	6.6	1.4
Sophomore	30,447	5.6	29,316	5.0	-3.7
Junior	35,966	6.6	35,689	6.1	-0.8
Senior	45,169	8.2	44,868	7.7	-0.7
Unspecified	37,187	6.8	44,845	7.7	20.6
Graduate	**238,497**	**43.5**	**264,749**	**45.4**	**11.0**
Master's	123,920	22.6	138,791	23.8	12.0
Doctoral	77,211	14.1	81,824	14.0	6.0
Professional Training	8,005	1.5	7,948	1.4	-0.7
Unspecified	29,361	5.4	36,185	6.2	23.2
Other	**54,941**	**10.0**	**57,168**	**9.8**	**4.1**
Practical Training	21,058	3.8	22,745	3.9	8.0
Non-Degree	12,168	2.2	14,013	2.4	15.2
Intensive English Lang.	21,716	4.0	20,410	3.5	-6.0
TOTAL	**547,867**	**100.0**	**582,996**	**100.0**	**6.4**

18   INTERNATIONAL STUDENTS BY ACADEMIC LEVEL, 2000/01 & 2001/02

Year	Under-graduate	Graduate	Other
1954/55	19,101	12,118	3,012
1959/60	25,164	18,910	4,412
1964/65	38,130	35,096	8,774
1969/70	63,296	59,112	12,551
1975/76	95,949	83,395	18,073
1979/80	172,378	94,207	19,758
1984/85	197,741	122,476	21,895
1987/88	176,669	156,366	23,152
1988/89	172,551	165,590	28,209
1989/90	184,527	169,827	32,495
1990/91	189,900	182,130	35,500
1991/92	197,070	191,330	31,190
1992/93	210,080	193,330	35,210
1993/94	213,610	201,030	35,110

19   INTERNATIONAL STUDENTS BY ACADEMIC LEVEL,
SELECTED YEARS 1954/55 – 2001/02

Year	Under-graduate	Graduate	Other
1994/95	221,500	191,738	39,396
1995/96	218,620	190,092	45,075
1996/97	218,743	190,244	48,997
1997/98	223,276	207,510	50,494
1998/99	235,802	211,426	43,706
1999/00	237,211	218,219	59,293
2000/01	254,429	238,497	54,941
2001/02	261,079	264,749	57,168

19 (cont'd) INTERNATIONAL STUDENTS BY ACADEMIC LEVEL, SELECTED YEARS 1954/55 – 2001/02

Characteristic	% Under-graduate	% Graduate	% Other
Sex			
Male	53.0	61.6	52.9
Female	47.0	38.4	47.1
Marital Status			
Single	93.9	77.5	83.6
Married	6.1	22.5	16.4
Enrollment Status			
Full-Time	89.0	86.2	84.0
Part-Time	11.0	13.8	16.0
Visa Type			
F Visa	87.5	86.1	79.4
J Visa	3.1	6.3	9.9
M Visa	0.2	0.0	0.5
Other Visa	9.2	7.6	10.3
Primary Source of Funds			
Personal & Family	80.4	51.5	70.6
U.S. College or University	9.2	37.9	7.0
Home Gov't/University	3.5	3.9	3.6
U.S. Private Sponsor	3.5	1.8	1.9
Foreign Private Sponsor	2.2	1.9	1.8

Characteristic	% Under-graduate	% Graduate	% Other
Current Employment	0.2	1.5	13.7
Other Sources	0.2	0.2	0.4
U.S. Government	0.5	0.9	0.5
International Organization	0.2	0.5	0.5
Field of Study			
Agriculture	0.7	2.1	1.4
Business & Management	23.3	17.4	11.5
Education	1.7	3.5	3.7
Engineering	10.9	21.4	4.9
Fine & Applied Arts	7.5	4.9	2.6
Health Professions	3.2	5.2	2.8
Humanities	2.1	4.4	2.0
Math & Computer Sciences	13.5	14.1	6.0
Physical & Life Sciences	4.3	10.6	2.5
Social Sciences	7.3	9.0	3.3
Other	14.8	6.2	6.0
Intensive English	1.3	0.1	38.9
Undeclared	9.4	1.1	14.5
NUMBER OF STUDENTS	261,079	264,749	57,168

20 PERSONAL & ACADEMIC CHARACTERISTICS BY ACADEMIC LEVEL, 2001/02

Year	% Male	% Female	% Single	% F Visa	% J Visa	% Other Visa Type	% Refugee*	Int'l Students
1976/77	69.2	30.8	73.7	75.0	10.4	7.3	7.3	203,068
1977/78	75.0	25.0	77.4	78.8	9.3	6.9	5.0	235,509
1978/79	74.1	25.9	74.7	80.7	9.8	5.7	3.8	263,938
1979/80	72.4	27.6	78.6	82.0	7.6	6.4	4.0	286,343
1980/81	71.7	28.3	80.1	82.9	6.7	5.6	4.8	311,882
1981/82	71.0	29.0	79.3	84.3	6.8	4.9	4.0	326,299
1982/83	70.9	29.1	80.1	84.0	7.2	5.2	3.6	336,985
1983/84	70.6	29.4	80.1	83.2	8.2	5.2	3.4	338,894
1984/85	69.8	30.2	80.4	83.5	8.4	5.1	3.0	342,113
1985/86	70.7	29.3	80.0	81.5	9.2	5.7	3.6	343,777
1986/87	68.9	31.1	79.7	81.0	11.0	5.2	2.8	349,609
1987/88	67.7	32.3	79.8	79.4	12.1	6.1	2.3	356,187
1988/89	66.5	33.5	80.9	79.0	12.5	6.5	2.0	366,354
1989/90	66.1	33.9	80.1	78.5	12.7	6.4	2.4	386,851
1990/91	64.0	36.0	78.5	80.6	11.0	6.4	2.0	407,529
1991/92	63.7	36.3	80.7	84.6	9.5	6.0	.	419,585
1992/93	63.0	37.0	82.5	85.5	8.5	6.1	.	438,618
1993/94	62.1	37.9	83.1	86.4	7.7	5.9	.	449,749
1994/95	60.9	39.1	83.4	85.8	7.7	6.4	.	452,635
1995/96	58.9	41.1	82.6	84.9	7.7	7.3	.	453,787
1996/97	59.0	41.0	84.4	85.6	6.8	7.6	.	457,984
1997/98	58.1	41.9	83.6	86.8	6.7	6.5	.	481,280
1998/99	58.0	42.0	85.2	87.3	6.3	6.4	.	490,933
1999/00	57.5	42.5	84.2	85.6	5.8	8.6	.	514,723
2000/01	57.1	42.9	84.7	85.8	5.8	8.4	.	547,867
2001/02	57.0	43.0	86.0	86.2	5.1	8.7	.	582,996

*After 1990, IIE ceased to collect data on refugee students.

21 PERSONAL CHARACTERISTICS, SELECTED YEARS 1976/77 – 2001/02

STUDY ABROAD

IN THIS SECTION

PERCENT OF U.S. STUDY ABROAD STUDENTS

Host Region	1985/86	1987/88	1989/90	1991/92	1993/94	1994/95	1995/96	1996/97	1997/98	1998/99	1999/00	2000/01
Africa	1.1	1.2	1.3	1.8	1.9	2.2	2.3	2.6	2.7	2.8	2.8	2.9
Asia	5.4	6.1	5.0	5.9	6.5	6.4	6.4	6.1	6.0	6.0	6.2	6.0
Europe	79.6	75.4	76.7	71.3	67.4	65.5	64.8	64.5	63.7	62.7	62.4	63.1
Latin America	7.0	9.2	9.4	12.3	13.4	13.7	15.4	15.3	15.6	15.0	14.0	14.5
Middle East	4.0	4.7	2.7	2.7	2.8	3.3	2.1	1.9	2.0	2.8	2.9	1.1
North America	0.9	1.4	0.8	0.9	0.7	0.7	0.7	0.7	0.9	0.7	0.9	0.7
Oceania	0.9	1.2	1.9	3.1	3.4	4.3	4.4	4.4	4.4	4.9	5.0	6.0
Multiple Regions	1.0	0.8	2.2	2.1	3.8	3.8	4.0	4.6	4.8	5.2	5.8	5.6
Students Reported	**48,483**	**62,341**	**70,727**	**71,154**	**76,302**	**84,403**	**89,242**	**99,448**	**113,959**	**129,770**	**143,590**	**154,168**

22 HOST REGIONS OF U.S. STUDY ABROAD STUDENTS, SELECTED YEARS 1985/86 — 2000/01

Region/ Locality	Total 1999/00	Total 2000/01	% Change	Region/ Locality	Total 1999/00	Total 2000/01	% Change
AFRICA	**3,969**	**4,540**	**14.4**	Equatorial Guinea	0	8	-
Africa, Unspecified	30	1	-96.7	Gabon	1	2	100.0
East Africa	**1,307**	**1,552**	**18.7**	**North Africa**	**601**	**751**	**25.0**
Eritrea	0	18	-	Canary Islands	22	0	-100.0
Ethiopia	0	12	-	Egypt	388	436	12.4
Kenya	695	846	21.7	Morocco	132	245	85.6
Madagascar	48	51	6.3	Western Sahara	0	1	-
Malawi	3	30	900.0	Tunisia	59	69	16.9
Mauritius	0	4	-				
Mozambique	12	66	450.0	**Southern Africa**	**969**	**1,225**	**26.4**
Reunion	1	4	300.0	Botswana	14	44	214.3
Rwanda	1	0	-100.0	Namibia	48	38	-20.8
Tanzania	253	295	16.6	South Africa	899	1,107	23.1
Uganda	44	28	-36.4	Swaziland	8	31	287.5
Zambia	0	11	-	Southern Africa, Unspec.	0	5	-
Zimbabwe	250	186	-25.6				
East Africa, Unspecified	0	1	-	**West Africa**	**1,006**	**893**	**-11.2**
				Benin	20	21	5.0
Central Africa	**56**	**118**	**110.7**	Burkina Faso	22	10	-54.5
Cameroon	53	95	79.2	Côte d'Ivoire	7	10	42.9
Central African Republic	0	13	-	Gambia	13	23	76.9
Chad	1	0	-100.0	Ghana	630	607	-3.7
Congo	1	0	-100.0	Guinea	1	0	-100.0

23 HOST REGIONS AND COUNTRIES OF U.S. STUDY ABROAD STUDENTS, ACADEMIC YEAR 1999/00 & 2000/01

Region/ Locality	Total 1999/00	Total 2000/01	% Change	Region/ Locality	Total 1999/00	Total 2000/01	% Change
Liberia	3	0	-100.0	**Eastern Europe**	**3,526**	**3,695**	**4.8**
Mali	82	57	-30.5	Albania	42	0	-100.0
Mauritania	1	2	100.0	Armenia	0	7	-
Niger	14	14	0.0	Azerbaijan	1	0	-100.0
Nigeria	26	5	-80.8	Belarus	16	0	-100.0
Senegal	180	140	-22.2	Bosnia & Herzegovina	4	19	375.0
Togo	5	4	-20.0	Bulgaria	15	30	100.0
West Africa, Unspecified	2	0	-100.0	Croatia	94	42	-55.3
				Czech Republic	1,248	1,273	2.0
ASIA	**8,834**	**9,247**	**4.7**	Estonia	11	18	63.6
				Georgia	0	1	-
East Asia	**6,585**	**6,778**	**2.9**	Hungary	441	439	-0.5
China	2,949	2,942	-0.2	Latvia	14	14	0.0
Hong Kong	342	470	37.4	Lithuania	23	23	0.0
Japan	2,679	2,618	-2.3	Macedonia	4	3	-25.0
Korea, Republic of	444	522	17.6	Moldova	1	0	-100.0
Macao	0	5	-	Poland	244	273	11.9
Mongolia	2	39	1,850.0	Romania	75	71	-5.3
Taiwan	169	182	7.7	Russia	1,103	1,152	4.4
				Slovakia	12	26	116.7
South/Central Asia	**1,285**	**1,259**	**-2.0**	Slovenia	34	20	-41.2
Bangladesh	21	49	133.3	Ukraine	77	132	71.4
Bhutan	1	0	-100.0	Yugoslavia, Former	53	70	32.1
India	811	750	-7.5	Eastern Europe, Unspec.	14	82	485.7
Kazakhstan	2	2	0.0				
Kyrgyzstan	9	0	-100.0	**Western Europe**	**86,016**	**93,199**	**8.4**
Nepal	389	395	1.5	Austria	2,246	2,396	6.7
Pakistan	3	3	0.0	Belgium	823	670	-18.6
Sri Lanka	46	59	28.3	Denmark	718	817	13.8
Tajikistan	1	0	-100.0	Finland	211	182	-13.7
Uzbekistan	2	1	-50.0	France	11,924	11,905	-0.2
				Germany	4,744	5,116	7.8
Southeast Asia	**964**	**1,210**	**25.5**	Gibraltar	1	0	-100.0
Cambodia	12	9	-25.0	Greece	1,449	1,754	21.0
Indonesia	189	213	12.7	Iceland	75	123	64.0
Laos	1	2	100.0	Ireland	3,810	3,973	4.3
Malaysia	26	77	196.2	Italy	12,930	16,127	24.7
Myanmar	1	0	-100.0	Liechtenstein	1	0	-100.0
Philippines	107	108	0.9	Luxembourg	462	407	-11.9
Singapore	87	117	34.5	Malta	72	118	63.9
Thailand	399	496	24.3	Monaco	13	9	-30.8
Vietnam	142	188	32.4	Netherlands	1,545	1,635	5.8
				Norway	277	215	-22.4
EUROPE	**89,593**	**97,271**	**8.6**	Portugal	60	77	28.3
Europe, Unspecified	51	377	639.2	Spain	13,974	16,016	14.6

23 (cont'd) HOST REGIONS AND COUNTRIES OF U.S. STUDY ABROAD STUDENTS, ACADEMIC YEAR 1999/00 & 2000/01

Region/ Locality	Total 1999/00	Total 2000/01	% Change		Region/ Locality	Total 1999/00	Total 2000/01	% Change
Sweden	538	543	0.9		Colombia	44	13	-70.5
Switzerland	845	827	-2.1		Ecuador	1,286	1,311	1.9
United Kingdom	29,289	30,289	3.4		Guyana	17	1	-94.1
W. Europe, Unspec.	9	0	-100.0		Paraguay	34	47	38.2
					Peru	349	356	2.0
LATIN AMERICA	**20,116**	**22,387**	**11.3**		Suriname	2	0	-100.0
Latin America, Unspec.	14	13	-7.1		Uruguay	9	49	444.4
					Venezuela	339	206	-39.2
Caribbean	**2,811**	**3,286**	**16.9**					
Anguilla	26	23	-11.5		**MIDDLE EAST**	**4,127**	**1,659**	**-59.8**
Antigua	4	11	175.0		Bahrain	0	2	-
Bahamas	411	515	25.3		Cyprus	15	37	146.7
Barbados	131	147	12.2		Iran	0	1	-
British Virgin Islands	57	97	70.2		Israel	3,898	1,248	-68.0
Cayman Islands	39	61	56.4		Jordan	86	83	-3.5
Cuba	553	905	63.7		Kuwait	2	3	50.0
Dominica	22	12	-45.5		Lebanon	13	19	46.2
Dominican Republic	542	527	-2.8		Palestinian Authority	1	1	0.0
Grenada	15	14	-6.7		Saudi Arabia	2	1	-50.0
Guadeloupe	36	26	-27.8		Syria	5	3	-40.0
Haiti	65	58	-10.8		Turkey	99	234	136.4
Jamaica	548	462	-15.7		United Arab Emirates	5	5	0.0
Martinique	81	46	-43.2		Yemen	1	3	200.0
Netherlands Antilles	16	22	37.5		Middle East, Unspecified	0	19	-
St. Kitts-Nevis	35	20	-42.9					
St. Lucia	2	10	400.0		**NORTH AMERICA**	**1,342**	**1,108**	**-17.4**
St. Vincent	0	2	-		Bermuda	67	68	1.5
Trinidad & Tobago	121	123	1.7		Canada	1,275	1,040	-18.4
Turks & Caicos Islands	9	9	0.0					
Caribbean, Unspecified	98	196	100.0		**OCEANIA**	**7,231**	**9,302**	**28.6**
					Australia	6,329	8,066	27.4
C. America/Mexico	**12,414**	**13,677**	**10.2**		Cook Islands	1	1	0.0
Belize	568	556	-2.1		Fed. Sts. of Micronesia	2	1	-50.0
Costa Rica	3,421	3,641	6.4		Fiji	34	8	-76.5
El Salvador	77	78	1.3		French Polynesia	20	24	20.0
Guatemala	389	473	21.6		Marshall Islands	0	7	-
Honduras	309	311	0.6		New Zealand	799	1,120	40.2
Mexico	7,374	8,360	13.4		Papua New Guinea	2	10	400.0
Nicaragua	201	162	-19.4		Tonga	0	5	-
Panama	75	96	28.0		Vanuatu	0	2	-
					Western Samoa	26	35	34.6
South America	**4,877**	**5,411**	**10.9**		Pacific Islands, Unspec.	18	23	27.8
Argentina	985	1,258	27.7					
Bolivia	158	177	12.0		**MULTI-COUNTRY**	**8,373**	**8,650**	**3.3**
Brazil	717	760	6.0					
Chile	937	1,233	31.6		**TOTAL**	**143,590**	**154,168**	**7.4**

23 (cont d) HOST REGIONS AND COUNTRIES OF U.S. STUDY ABROAD STUDENTS, ACADEMIC YEAR 1999/00 & 2000/01

PERCENT OF U.S. STUDY ABROAD STUDENTS

Field of Study	1985/86	1987/88	1989/90	1991/92	1993/94	1994/95	1995/96	1996/97	1997/98*	1998/99	1999/00	2000/01	2000/01 Students
Social Sciences	-	-	-	-	-	-	-	-	-	20.3	20.1	20.3	31,302
Business & Management	10.9	11.1	10.9	12.0	13.6	13.5	13.9	14.6	15.6	17.7	17.7	18.1	27,938
Humanities	-	-	-	-	-	-	-	-	-	14.6	14.5	14.5	22,411
Fine or Applied Arts	6.9	6.4	6.1	9.9	7.7	9.0	6.8	7.1	7.7	8.0	8.6	8.5	13,120
Foreign Languages	16.7	14.8	12.5	14.0	11.3	10.3	10.7	9.3	8.0	8.1	8.2	8.2	12,694
Physical Sciences	3.8	2.5	3.7	3.8	5.3	6.8	6.8	6.8	7.0	7.4	7.4	7.1	10,970
Other	8.2	6.8	6.8	7.6	7.7	6.4	7.5	7.8	4.8	5.6	5.1	4.9	7,527
Undeclared	4.2	3.8	3.4	4.1	3.6	3.3	3.9	3.9	4.2	4.3	5.1	4.5	6,877
Education	4.1	4.0	4.6	5.7	4.0	3.8	3.7	4.3	4.5	4.2	4.2	4.4	6,710
Engineering	1.6	1.4	1.3	1.6	2.3	2.2	2.1	1.9	2.7	2.8	2.9	2.7	4,136
Health Sciences	1.7	1.4	1.1	1.1	1.7	2.1	2.3	2.7	3.2	3.8	2.8	3.2	4,894
Math & Computer Sciences	1.3	1.2	0.8	1.1	1.1	1.2	1.3	1.6	1.6	1.8	2.0	2.0	3,136
Agriculture	1.0	0.7	0.4	0.7	0.9	0.7	1.0	1.2	1.5	1.4	1.4	1.6	2,453
Soc. Sci. & Humanities	39.7	45.9	48.4	38.4	37.1	36.6	35.2	34.0	34.8	-	-	-	-
Dual Major	-	-	-	-	3.6	4.1	4.7	4.9	4.3	-	-	-	-
Total	**100.0**	**100.0**	**100.0**	**100.0**	**100.0**	**100.0**	**100.0**	**100.0**	**100.0**	**100.0**	**100.0**		**154,168**

*Social Sciences and Humanities were combined until 1998/99.

24 FIELDS OF STUDY OF U.S. STUDY ABROAD STUDENTS, SELECTED YEARS 1985/86 —2000/01

PERCENT OF STUDY ABROAD STUDENTS

Duration	1985/86	1987/88	1989/90	1991/92	1993/94	1994/95	1995/96	1996/97	1997/98	1998/99	1999/00	2000/01	2000/01 Students
One Semester	37.3	35.0	35.2	37.5	37.2	39.4	39.4	40.2	38.4	39.8	38.1	38.5	59,412
Summer Term	28.1	32.4	33.9	30.8	30.9	30.0	31.4	32.8	33.8	34.6	34.2	33.7	51,979
Fewer Than 8 Weeks	-	-	-	-	1.7	2.5	3.5	3.3	4.2	4.8	7.3	7.4	11,364
Academic Year	17.7	17.5	15.9	15.9	14.3	14.0	12.1	10.7	9.5	8.6	8.2	7.3	11,218
January Term	-	-	-	-	5.6	6.9	5.6	6.8	6.6	6.5	6.0	7.0	10,718
One Quarter	7.9	7.3	6.4	9.7	6.3	4.8	5.1	4.0	4.8	4.0	4.7	4.1	6,348
Other	7.7	7.4	7.9	5.5	1.4	0.9	1.3	1.2	1.0	0.8	0.4	0.9	1,321
Calendar Year	1.1	0.4	0.7	0.6	0.5	0.5	0.7	0.2	0.5	0.2	0.4	0.6	940
Two Quarters	-	-	-	-	2.0	1.1	0.9	0.9	1.1	0.6	0.7	0.6	868
Total	**100.0**	**100.0**	**100.0**	**100.0**	**100.0**	**100.0**	**100.0**	**100.0**	**100.0**	**100.0**	**100.0**	**100.0**	**154,168**

25 DURATION OF U.S. STUDY ABROAD, SELECTED YEARS 1985/86 —2000/01

	1993/94	1994/95	1995/96	1996/97	1997/98	1998/99	1999/00	2000/01	2000/01 Students
Academic level									
Junior	40.6	43.0	41.6	41.3	42.2	40.3	39.8	38.9	60,032
Senior	15.6	16.3	16.2	18.3	17.7	19.0	17.7	20.0	30,893
Bachelor's, Unspecified	19.1	17.5	18.1	14.7	13.2	13.3	15.6	13.5	20,865
Sophomore	11.8	10.8	12.1	12.8	13.4	13.2	13.6	14.0	21,608
Master's	4.0	4.1	3.7	4.2	5.1	4.5	5.0	4.5	6,960
Graduate, Unspecified	2.3	2.6	3.2	3.3	2.6	3.2	2.7	3.1	4,845
Freshman	3.5	2.5	2.0	2.4	2.7	2.5	3.2	3.1	4,803
Associate	1.6	1.3	2.0	1.9	2.3	2.5	0.9	0.9	1,354
Other	0.8	1.5	0.7	0.8	0.5	1.1	1.0	1.1	1,658
Doctoral	0.7	0.5	0.4	0.3	0.4	0.5	0.6	0.7	1,150
Total	**100.0**	**100.0**	**100.0**	**100.0**	**100.0**	**100.0**	**100.0**	**100.0**	**154,168**
Sex									
Female	62.9	62.2	65.3	64.9	64.8	65.2	64.6	65.0	100,170
Male	37.1	37.8	34.7	35.1	35.2	34.8	35.4	35.0	53,998
Total	**100.0**	**100.0**	**100.0**	**100.0**	**100.0**	**100.0**	**100.0**	**100.0**	**154,168**
Race/Ethnicity									
Caucasian	83.8	86.4	84.4	83.9	84.5	85.0	83.7	84.3	129,983
Hispanic-American	5.0	4.5	5.0	5.1	5.5	5.2	5.0	5.4	8,383
Asian-American	5.0	4.9	5.1	5.0	4.8	4.4	4.8	5.4	8,344
African-American	2.8	2.8	2.9	3.5	3.8	3.3	3.5	3.5	5,404
Multiracial	3.1	1.1	2.3	2.1	0.8	1.2	0.9	0.9	1,322
Native American	0.3	0.3	0.3	0.3	0.6	0.9	0.5	0.5	731
Visa Students	-	-	-	-	-	-	1.6	-	-
TOTAL	**100.0**	**100.0**	**100.0**	**100.0**	**100.0**	**100.0**	**100.0**	**100.0**	**154,168**

26   PROFILE OF U.S. STUDY ABROAD STUDENTS, 1993/94 – 2000/01

Carnegie Category	1993/94 %	1994/95 %	1995/96 %	1996/97 %	1997/98 %	1998/99 %	1999/00 %	2000/01 %	2000/01 Average	2000/01 Students
Research I&II	40.2	41.1	43.6	42.8	42.0	42.3	43.8	43.0	571	66,222
Master's I&II	19.0	18.5	19.0	20.7	20.2	20.3	20.1	20.7	100	31,894
Baccalaureate I&II	20.8	21.5	21.2	20.6	20.7	20.5	19.1	18.7	89	28,847
Doctoral I&II	14.9	14.5	12.2	11.9	12.6	12.5	12.5	13.3	230	20,493
Associate	2.9	2.3	2.6	2.4	2.8	2.7	2.5	2.6	29	3,941
Other Institutions	2.2	2.1	1.5	1.7	1.8	1.7	2.0	1.8	32	2,771
Total	**100.0**	**100.0**	**100.0**	**100.0**	**100.0**	**100.0**	**100.0**	**100.0**		**154,168**

For-Credit Internships or Work Abroad by Carnegie Type	1998/99 %	1998/99 Students	1998/99 Number of Schools	1999/00 %	1999/00 Students	1999/00 Number of Schools	2000/01 %	2000/01 Schools	2000/01 Number of Schools
Research I&II	40.6	2,152	36	45.7	2,554	48	40.0	2,779	53
Doctoral I&II	11.8	627	24	8.6	483	30	11.0	767	26
Master's I&II	16.5	876	83	18.5	1,033	97	21.2	1,475	102
Baccalaureate I&II	27.4	1,454	78	22.4	1,250	91	25.3	1,761	97
Associate	1.3	69	10	1.3	72	7	0.5	32	5
Other Institutions	2.4	126	10	3.4	192	12	2.0	136	13
Total		**5304**	**241**		**5,584**	**285**		**6,950**	**296**

Program Sponsorship	1993/94 %	1994/95 %	1995/96 %	1996/97 %	1997/98 %	1998/99 %	1999/00 %	2000/01 %	2000/01 Students
Solely own institution	73.4	71.2	71.9	72.9	74.1	73.9	73.9	72.3	111,489
Other institutions/organizations	26.6	28.8	28.1	27.1	25.9	26.1	26.1	27.7	42,679
Total	**100.0**	**100.0**	**100.0**	**100.0**	**100.0**	**100.0**	**100.0**	**100.0**	**154,168**

Institutional Financial Support	1993/94 % of Respondents	1994/95 % of Respondents	1995/96 % of Respondents	1996/97 % of Respondents	1997/98 % of Respondents	1998/99 % of Respondents	1999/00 % of Respondents	2000/01 % of Respondents	2000/01 Reporting Institutions
a) Aid for all institutionally approved study abroad programs	46.2	62.3	54.0	54.6	57.3	55.4	57.8	55.8	456
b) Aid for institutionally approved study abroad programs but not other study abroad programs	17.0	12.0	16.2	15.9	17.9	18.8	19.6	21.4	175
c) Other	11.4	7.9	10.6	10.1	4.7	6.6	7.4	5.0	41
d) Do not know	16.2	1.6	8.7	8.9	9.5	8.0	6.3	6.4	52
e) Federal or state aid but no institutional aid	7.2	6.5	7.8	7.5	7.3	8.0	6.2	6.7	55
f) Federal aid but not state or institutional aid	2.0	9.8	2.7	3.0	3.4	3.2	2.7	1.8	15
Total	**100.0**	**100.0**	**100.0**	**100.0**	**100.0**	**100.0**	**100.0**	**100.0**	**794**
Number of Responding Institutions	**631**	**573**	**772**	**790**	**770**	**787**	**789**	**789**	**794**

27 HOME INSTITUTIONAL TYPE, FOR-CREDIT INTERNSHIPS OR WORK ABROAD, PROGRAM SPONSORSHIP, AND FINANCIAL SUPPORT FOR U.S. STUDY ABROAD STUDENTS, 1993/94 — 2000/01

Rank	Institution	City	State	Study Abroad Students	Total Number of Degrees Conferred IPEDS 2000	Estimated % Participation In Study Abroad
1	University of Notre Dame	Notre Dame	IN	1,133	2,890	39.2
2	Yeshiva University	New York	NY	608	1,566	38.8
3	Cornell University	Ithaca	NY	974	3,452	28.2
4	Duke University	Durham	NC	895	3,376	26.5
4	Georgetown University	Washington	DC	1,003	3,792	26.5
6	University of Delaware	Newark	DE	1,064	4,208	25.3
7	Brown University	Providence	RI	524	2,085	25.1
8	Tulane University	New Orleans	LA	684	2,929	23.4
9	University of Kansas Main Campus	Lawrence	KS	1,141	5,025	22.7
10	Tufts University	Medford	MA	526	2,469	21.3
10	Brandeis University	Waltham	MA	233	1,094	21.3
12	Emory University	Atlanta	GA	672	3,181	21.1
13	University of North Carolina at Chapel Hill	Chapel Hill	NC	1,286	6,123	21.0
14	Syracuse University	Syracuse	NY	861	4,222	20.4
15	University of Pennsylvania	Philadelphia	PA	1,231	6,087	20.2
16	University of Vermont	Burlington	VT	451	2,246	20.1
17	Georgia Institute of Technology	Atlanta	GA	641	3,263	19.6
18	Florida State University	Tallahassee	FL	1,464	7,607	19.3
19	Michigan State University	East Lansing	MI	1,835	9,549	19.2
20	University of Georgia	Athens	GA	1,229	6,699	18.4

28A   LEADING INSTITUTIONS BY ESTIMATED PARTICIPATION IN STUDY ABROAD: TOP 20 RESEARCH INSTITUTIONS, 2000/01

Rank	Institution	City	State	Study Abroad Students
1	Michigan State University	East Lansing	MI	1,835
2	University of Texas at Austin	Austin	TX	1,633
3	New York University	New York	NY	1,471
4	Florida State University	Tallahassee	FL	1,464
5	University of Illinois at Urbana-Champaign	Champaign	IL	1,369
6	University of North Carolina at Chapel Hill	Chapel Hill	NC	1,286
7	Indiana University at Bloomington	Bloomington	IN	1,268
8	University of Wisconsin - Madison	Madison	WI	1,253
9	Arizona State University Main	Tempe	AZ	1,248
10	Brigham Young University	Provo	UT	1,235
11	University of Pennsylvania	Philadelphia	PA	1,231
12	University of Georgia	Athens	GA	1,229
13	University of Arizona	Tucson	AZ	1,214
14	The Ohio State University Main Campus	Columbus	OH	1,201
15	University of Minnesota -Twin Cities	Minneapolis	MN	1,199

28B   LEADING INSTITUTIONS BY TOTAL NUMBER OF STUDY ABROAD STUDENTS: TOP 20 RESEARCH INSTITUTIONS, 2000/01

Rank	Institution	City	State	Study Abroad Students
16	University of Southern California	Los Angeles	CA	1,160
17	University of Kansas Main Campus	Lawrence	KS	1,141
18	University of Notre Dame	Notre Dame	IN	1,133
19	Penn State University Park	University Park	PA	1,124
20	University of Florida	Gainesville	FL	1,092

28B **(cont'd) LEADING INSTITUTIONS BY TOTAL NUMBER OF STUDY ABROAD STUDENTS: TOP 20 RESEARCH INSTITUTIONS, 2000/01**

Rank	Institution	City	State	Study Abroad Students	Total Number of Degrees Conferred IPEDS 2000	Estimated % Participation In Study Abroad
1	Dartmouth College	Hanover	NH	625	1,466	42.6
2	Worcester Polytechnic Institute	Worcester	MA	291	872	33.4
3	Baylor University	Waco	TX	996	3,046	32.7
3	Wake Forest University	Winston-Salem	NC	529	1,619	32.7
5	Miami University	Oxford	OH	1,348	4,430	30.4
6	College of William and Mary	Williamsburg	VA	520	2,032	25.6
7	Pepperdine University	Malibu	CA	619	2,638	23.5
8	Texas Christian University	Fort Worth	TX	354	1,585	22.3
9	Boston College	Chestnut Hill	MA	854	3,982	21.5
10	University of San Diego	San Diego	CA	425	2,006	21.2
11	University of Denver	Denver	CO	466	2,450	19.0
12	American University	Washington	DC	493	2,821	17.5
13	George Mason University	Fairfax	VA	792	5,045	15.7
14	Southern Methodist University	Dallas	TX	383	2,498	15.3
15	Biola University	La Mirada	CA	113	759	14.9
16	Loyola University of Chicago	Chicago	IL	459	3,215	14.3
17	University of New Hampshire	Durham	NH	453	3,282	13.8
18	Duquesne University	Pittsburgh	PA	323	2,355	13.7
18	Colorado School of Mines	Golden	CO	95	696	13.7
20	Ball State University	Muncie	IN	510	3,819	13.4

29A **LEADING INSTITUTIONS BY ESTIMATED PARTICIPATION IN STUDY ABROAD: TOP 20 DOCTORAL INSTITUTIONS, 2000/01**

Rank	Institution	City	State	Study Abroad Students
1	Miami University	Oxford	OH	1,348
2	Baylor University	Waco	TX	996
3	Boston College	Chestnut Hill	MA	854
4	George Mason University	Fairfax	VA	792
5	San Diego State University	San Diego	CA	639
6	Dartmouth College	Hanover	NH	625
7	Pepperdine University	Malibu	CA	619
8	Wake Forest University	Winston-Salem	NC	529
9	College of William & Mary	Williamsburg	VA	520
10	Ball State University	Muncie	IN	510
11	American University	Washington	DC	493
12	University of Denver	Denver	CO	466
13	Loyola University of Chicago	Chicago	IL	459
14	University of New Hampshire	Durham	NH	453
15	Western Michigan University	Kalamazoo	MI	446
16	University of San Diego	San Diego	CA	425
17	Florida International University	Miami	FL	405
18	Southern Methodist University	Dallas	TX	383
19	Binghamton University – SUNY	Binghamton	NY	360
20	Texas Christian University	Fort Worth	TX	354

29B   LEADING INSTITUTIONS BY TOTAL NUMBER OF STUDY ABROAD STUDENTS: TOP 20 DOCTORAL INSTITUTIONS, 2000/01

Rank	Institution	City	State	Study Abroad Students	Total Number of Degrees Conferred IPEDS 2000	Estimated % Participation In Study Abroad
1	Elon University	Elon College	NC	710	818	86.8
2	Linfield College	McMinnville	OR	222	354	62.7
3	Calvin College	Grand Rapids	MI	486	870	55.9
4	West Virginia Wesleyan College	Buckhannon	WV	137	280	48.9
5	University of Evansville	Evansville	IN	302	665	45.4
6	Truman State University	Kirksville	MO	502	1,261	39.8
7	Whitworth College	Spokane	WA	165	498	33.1
8	Centenary College of Louisiana	Shreveport	LA	62	193	32.1
9	University of Richmond	Richmond	VA	322	1,044	30.8
10	Pacific Lutheran University	Tacoma	WA	299	988	30.3
11	Fresno Pacific University	Fresno	CA	60	205	29.3
12	Baker University	Baldwin City	KS	47	164	28.7
13	University of Saint Thomas	St. Paul	MN	682	2,401	28.4
14	Trinity University	San Antonio	TX	172	620	27.7

30A   LEADING INSTITUTIONS BY ESTIMATED PARTICIPATION IN STUDY ABROAD: TOP 20 MASTER'S INSTITUTIONS, 2000/01

Rank	Institution	City	State	Study Abroad Students	Total Number of Degrees Conferred IPEDS 2000	Estimated % Participation In Study Abroad
15	Saint Michael's College	Colchester	VT	157	577	27.2
16	Mary Washington College	Fredericksburg	VA	212	801	26.5
17	University of Portland	Portland	OR	196	754	26.0
18	Ithaca College	Ithaca	NY	352	1,445	24.4
19	Suffolk University	Boston	MA	360	1,604	22.4
20	Rollins College	Winter Park	FL	188	842	22.3

30A   (cont'd) LEADING INSTITUTIONS BY ESTIMATED PARTICIPATION IN STUDY ABROAD: TOP 20 MASTER'S INSTITUTIONS, 2000/01

Rank	Institution	City	State	Study Abroad Students
1	Elon University	Elon College	NC	710
2	University of Saint Thomas	St. Paul	MN	682
3	James Madison University	Harrisonburg	VA	658
4	University of Northern Iowa	Cedar Falls	IA	577
5	California Polytechnic State U. – San Luis Obispo	San Luis Obispo	CA	556
6	Truman State University	Kirksville	MO	502
7	Calvin College	Grand Rapids	MI	486
8	Villanova University	Villanova	PA	449
9	Appalachian State University	Boone	NC	436
10	Western Washington University	Bellingham	WA	418
11	University of Dayton	Dayton	OH	382
12	Loyola College in Maryland	Baltimore	MD	377
13	College of Charleston	Charleston	SC	361
14	Suffolk University	Boston	MA	360
15	Grand Valley State University	Allendale	MI	355
16	Ithaca College	Ithaca	NY	352
17	University of Wisconsin – Eau Claire	Eau Claire	WI	345
18	San Francisco State University	San Francisco	CA	332
19	University of Richmond	Richmond	VA	322
20	University of Wisconsin – Stevens Point	Stevens Point	WI	310

30B   LEADING INSTITUTIONS BY TOTAL NUMBER OF STUDY ABROAD STUDENTS: TOP 20 MASTER'S INSTITUTIONS, 2000/01

Rank	Institution	City	State	Study Abroad Students	Total Number of Degrees Conferred IPEDS 2000	Estimated % Participation In Study Abroad
1	College of St. Benedict/St. John's U.	St. Joseph/Collegeville	MN	657	466	141.0 *
2	Antioch University	Yellow Springs	OH	131	100	131.0 *
3	Wofford College	Spartanburg	SC	279	253	110.3 *
4	Kalamazoo College	Kalamazoo	MI	317	299	106.0 *
5	Saint Olaf College	Northfield	MN	660	670	98.5
6	Goshen College	Goshen	IN	219	223	98.2
7	Austin College	Sherman	TX	345	352	98.0
8	DePauw University	Greencastle	IN	491	506	97.0
9	Principia College	Elsah	IL	112	121	92.6
10	Centre College	Danville	KY	202	236	85.6
11	Earlham College	Richmond	IN	219	259	84.6
12	Dickinson College	Carlisle	PA	342	410	83.4
13	Lafayette College	Easton	PA	420	518	81.1
14	Carleton College	Northfield	MN	342	425	80.5
15	Bates College	Lewiston	ME	362	467	77.5
16	Berea College	Berea	KY	194	253	76.7
17	Colby College	Waterville	ME	365	478	76.4
18	Colgate University	Hamilton	NY	503	663	75.9
19	Hartwick College	Oneonta	NY	220	294	74.8
20	Central College	Pella	IA	148	200	74.0

* Estimated participation may exceed 100% of conferred degrees if students enroll for multiple sojourns during their college experience.

**31A   LEADING INSTITUTIONS BY ESTIMATED PARTICIPATION IN STUDY ABROAD:
TOP 20 BACCALAUREATE INSTITUTIONS, 2000/01**

Rank	Institution	City	State	Study Abroad Students
1	Saint Olaf College	Northfield	MN	660
2	College of Saint Benedict/Saint John's University	St. Joseph/Collegeville	MN	657
3	Colgate University	Hamilton	NY	503
4	DePauw University	Green Castle	IN	491
5	Lafayette College	Easton	PA	420
6	Messiah College	Grantham	PA	403
7	Middlebury College	Middlebury	VT	402
8	Gustavus Adolphus College	St. Peter	MN	397
9	Wesleyan University	Middletown	CT	374
10	Colby College	Waterville	ME	365
11	Bates College	Lewiston	ME	362
12	Bucknell University	Lewisburg	PA	359
13	Smith College	Northampton	MA	358
14	Colorado College	Colorado Springs	CO	357
15	Austin College	Sherman	TX	345
16	Dickinson College	Carlisle	PA	342
16	Carleton College	Northfield	MN	342
16	Wellesley College	Wellesley	MA	342
19	Concordia College – Moorhead	Moorhead	MN	337
20	Union College	Schenectady	NY	332

**31B   LEADING INSTITUTIONS BY TOTAL NUMBER OF STUDY ABROAD STUDENTS:
TOP 20 BACCALAUREATE INSTITUTIONS, 2000/01**

INTENSIVE ENGLISH

% of Students Intending Further Study	Number of Programs	Average Number of Students Per Program	Total Students All Programs	Average Number of Student-Weeks Per Program	Total Student-Weeks All Programs
30% and less	38	692	26,281	6,314	239,943
40% to 60%	43	392	16,854	5,079	218,403
70% and more	66	258	17,031	3,468	228,907
All reporting programs*	147	409	60,166	4,675	687,253
All programs	196		78,521		865,603

*49 programs did not provide further study data.

32 IEP STUDENTS AND STUDENT-WEEKS BY THE PERCENTAGE OF STUDENTS INTENDING TO CONTINUE FURTHER (Non-IEP) STUDY IN THE U.S., 2001

Rank	Place of Origin	2000 Total Students	2001 Total Students	% Change 2000-2001	% of IEP Total Students	2000 Student-Weeks	2001 Student-Weeks	% Change 2000-2001
	WORLD TOTAL	85,238	78,521	-7.9		866,715	865,603	-0.1
1	Japan	19,585	16,470	-15.9	21.0	201,246	187,500	-6.8
2	Korea, Republic of	12,772	13,110	2.6	16.7	157,379	175,218	11.3
3	Taiwan	9,325	7,605	-18.4	9.7	80,035	77,718	-2.9
4	Brazil	6,020	5,253	-12.7	6.7	43,028	41,254	-4.1
5	Mexico	2,797	4,369	56.2	5.6	27,718	43,907	58.4
6	Venezuela	2,614	2,487	-4.9	3.2	28,816	27,346	-5.1
7	Colombia	2,549	2,255	-11.5	2.9	32,147	27,132	-15.6
8	Turkey	2,118	2,254	6.4	2.9	24,032	24,264	1.0
9	Saudi Arabia	2,458	2,191	-10.9	2.8	31,879	29,674	-6.9
10	Thailand	2,009	1,929	-4.0	2.5	23,093	24,642	6.7
11	Italy	2,471	1,924	-22.1	2.5	12,736	11,296	-11.3
12	China	1,839	1,760	-4.3	2.2	20,886	22,052	5.6
13	France	1,683	1,587	-5.7	2.0	12,971	12,662	-2.4
14	Switzerland	1,494	1,584	6.0	2.0	13,399	13,529	1.0
15	Germany	1,332	1,396	4.8	1.8	11,960	13,326	11.4
16	Argentina	1,416	1,303	-8.0	1.7	10,098	9,215	-8.7
17	Spain	1,265	742	-41.3	0.9	7,815	6,401	-18.1
18	Chile	636	664	4.4	0.8	4,774	5,157	8.0
19	Indonesia	679	575	-15.3	0.7	7,567	6,275	-17.1
20	Peru	426	475	11.5	0.6	4,993	5,773	15.6

33 LEADING PLACES OF ORIGIN OF IEP STUDENTS, 2000 & 2001

Place of Origin	Total Students	Student-Weeks
AFRICA	**1,232**	**15,567**
East Africa	**86**	**1,121**
Burundi	3	51
Comoros	0	0
Eritrea	8	82
Ethiopia	14	240
Kenya	11	169
Madagascar	9	76
Malawi	1	7
Mauritius	0	0
Mozambique	3	28
Rwanda	9	76
Somalia	5	53
Tanzania	17	244
Uganda	3	71
Zambia	2	20
Zimbabwe	1	4
Central Africa	**161**	**2,075**
Angola	37	579
Cameroon	47	462
Central African Republic	2	13
Chad	3	35
Congo	27	357
Equatorial Guinea	7	134
Gabon	34	446
São Tomé & Príncipe	0	0
Zaire/Congo	4	49
North Africa	**441**	**5,338**
Algeria	19	222
Egypt	87	1,020
Libya	4	59
Morocco	238	2,733
Sudan	23	349
Tunisia	70	955
Southern Africa	**10**	**83**
Botswana	3	24
Namibia	2	21
South Africa	0	0
Swaziland	5	38

Place of Origin	Total Students	Student-Weeks
West Africa	**534**	**6,950**
Benin	12	213
Burkina Faso	10	125
Cape Verde	0	0
Côte d'Ivoire	122	1,330
Gambia	0	0
Ghana	4	50
Guinea	50	644
Guinea-Bissau	6	108
Liberia	3	41
Mali	75	991
Mauritania	32	367
Niger	54	761
Nigeria	13	148
Senegal	102	1,379
Sierra Leone	1	24
Togo	50	769
ASIA	**42,906**	**511,679**
East Asia	**39,429**	**467,543**
China	1,760	22,052
Hong Kong	356	3,619
Japan	16,470	187,500
Korea, Dem. People's Rep.	17	97
Korea, Republic of	13,110	175,218
Macao	23	323
Mongolia	88	1,016
Taiwan	7,605	77,718
South & Central Asia	**476**	**6,032**
Afghanistan	5	37
Bangladesh	24	338
Bhutan	1	16
India	96	1,193
Kazakhstan	76	775
Kyrgyzstan	33	230
Nepal	18	289
Pakistan	52	674
Sri Lanka	35	334
Tajikistan	35	774
Turkmenistan	8	30
Uzbekistan	93	1,342

Place of Origin	Total Students	Student-Weeks	Place of Origin	Total Students	Student-Weeks
Southeast Asia	**3,001**	**38,104**	Macedonia	10	82
Cambodia	36	484	Moldova	20	177
Indonesia	575	6,275	Poland	340	3,482
Laos	11	121	Romania	34	316
Malaysia	75	833	Russia	400	4,353
Myanmar	37	538	Slovakia	46	405
Philippines	53	582	Slovenia	25	93
Singapore	5	38	Ukraine	187	1,929
Thailand	1,929	24,642	Yugoslavia, Former	29	397
Vietnam	280	4,591			
			Western Europe	**8,368**	**68,776**
MIDDLE EAST	**6,032**	**75,482**	Andorra	1	4
Bahrain	37	473	Austria	292	2,589
Cyprus	26	254	Belgium	201	2,194
Iran	129	1,684	Denmark	83	655
Iraq	11	201	Finland	51	536
Israel	118	1,191	France	1,587	12,662
Jordan	66	956	Germany	1,396	13,326
Kuwait	210	3,097	Greece	37	627
Lebanon	116	1,336	Iceland	5	41
Oman	73	1,352	Ireland	0	0
Palestinian Authority	34	471	Italy	1,924	11,296
Qatar	144	2,076	Liechtenstein	3	24
Saudi Arabia	2,191	29,674	Luxembourg	1	4
Syria	81	920	Netherlands	156	1,895
Turkey	2,254	24,264	Norway	37	328
United Arab Emirates	456	6,739	Portugal	49	474
Yemen	86	794	San Marino	3	18
			Spain	742	6,401
EUROPE	**9,958**	**85,025**	Sweden	179	1,868
			Switzerland	1,584	13,529
Eastern Europe	**1,590**	**16,249**	United Kingdom	37	305
Albania	34	435	Vatican City	0	0
Armenia	9	121			
Azerbaijan	18	139	**LATIN AMERICA**	**18,265**	**176,680**
Belarus	23	288			
Bosnia & Herzegovina	28	334	**Caribbean**	**232**	**2,678**
Bulgaria	52	553	Antigua	0	0
Croatia	41	293	Aruba	0	0
Czech Republic	89	924	Bahamas	2	8
Estonia	22	216	British Virgin Islands	0	0
Georgia	18	168	Cuba	21	354
Hungary	65	534	Dominican Republic	164	1,845
Latvia	57	485	Grenada	0	0
Lithuania	43	525	Guadeloupe	7	65

34 (cont'd) REGIONS AND PLACES OF ORIGIN OF IEP STUDENTS, 2001

Place of Origin	Total Students	Student-Weeks		Place of Origin	Total Students	Student-Weeks
Haiti	38	406		Peru	475	5,773
Jamaica	0	0		Suriname	0	0
Martinique	0	0		Uruguay	39	298
Netherlands Antilles	0	0		Venezuela	2,487	27,346
St. Lucia	0	0		**NORTH AMERICA**	**87**	**734**
Central America/Mexico	**4,872**	**50,309**		Canada	87	734
Belize	10	51				
Costa Rica	85	961		**OCEANIA**	**25**	**287**
El Salvador	68	1,033		Australia	7	20
Guatemala	75	905		Cook Islands	0	0
Honduras	72	1,038		Federated States of Micronesia	2	30
Mexico	4,369	43,907		Fiji	0	0
Nicaragua	52	707		French Polynesia	4	28
Panama	141	1,707		Kiribati	2	32
				Marshall Islands	4	81
South America	**13,161**	**123,693**		New Caledonia	0	0
Argentina	1,303	9,215		New Zealand	2	32
Bolivia	118	1,528		Palau	2	32
Brazil	5,253	41,254		Tonga	1	16
Chile	664	5,157		Western Samoa	1	16
Colombia	2,255	27,132				
Ecuador	449	4,571		**STATELESS**	**10**	**148**
Falkland Islands	0	0				
Paraguay	118	1,419		**WORLD TOTAL**	**78,521**	**865,603**

34 (cont'd) **REGIONS AND PLACES OF ORIGIN OF IEP STUDENTS,** 2001

State	Reporting Programs	Total Students	Total Student-Weeks
Alabama	1	272	3,868
Arkansas	2	259	4,708
Arizona	0	0	0
California	40	26,925	247,102
Colorado	6	1,133	14,550
Connecticut	1	328	3,544
District of Columbia	4	1,021	11,886
Delaware	1	765	9,080
Florida	10	4,024	35,912
Georgia	2	1,137	14,594
Hawaii	3	1,175	20,025
Iowa	2	291	4,947
Illinois	7	1,938	23,330
Indiana	4	599	7,351
Kansas	3	662	10,580
Kentucky	2	438	4,918
Louisiana	2	235	1,513
Massachusetts	6	4,499	44,243
Maryland	3	551	10,754
Maine	1	43	540
Michigan	4	777	12,468
Minnesota	2	766	6,186
Missouri	4	333	5,225
Mississippi	3	350	5,532
North Carolina	3	743	10,134
North Dakota	1	32	410
Nebraska	2	448	9,906
New Jersey	2	407	4,572
New York	14	9,217	104,276
Ohio	6	1,141	15,849
Oklahoma	2	1,781	17,200
Oregon	7	1,056	12,635
Pennsylvania	5	1,502	18,040
South Carolina	1	307	4,921
South Dakota	1	5	75
Tennessee	6	1,133	18,205
Texas	10	5,956	78,390
Utah	5	837	10,604
Virginia	5	1,356	17,404
Vermont	1	290	2,742
Washington	8	2,829	26,660
Wisconsin	3	946	10,548
West Virginia	0	0	0
Wyoming	1	14	176
U.S. TOTAL	**196**	**78,521**	**865,603**

35 IEP STUDENTS BY STATE, 2001

CALIFORNIA		NEW YORK	
	% of Students		**% of Students**
Part-Time	8.4%	Part-Time	24.0%
Full-Time	91.6%	Full-Time	76.0%
State Totals	**26,925**	**State Totals**	**9,217**
	% Student-Weeks		**% Student-Weeks**
Part-Time	4.7%	Part-Time	23.4%
Full-Time	95.3%	Full-Time	76.6%
State Totals	**247,102**	**State Totals**	**104,276**

TEXAS		FLORIDA	
	% of Students		**% of Students**
Part-Time	61.5%	Part-Time	33.2%
Full-Time	38.5%	Full-Time	66.8%
State Totals	**5,956**	**State Totals**	**4,024**
	% Student-Weeks		**% Student-Weeks**
Part-Time	49.1%	Part-Time	12.9%
Full-Time	50.9%	Full-Time	87.1%
State Totals	**78,390**	**State Totals**	**35,912**

*Full-time enrollment is 18 class-hours a week or more, while part-time study is less than 18 class-hours.

36 IEP STUDENTS AND STUDENT-WEEKS BY ENROLLMENT STATUS IN SELECTED LEADING STATES, 2001

CALIFORNIA

Rank	Place of Origin	Students	Student-Weeks	% of Students
1	Japan	7,409	69,705	27.5
2	Korea, Republic of	3,815	42,088	14.2
3	Taiwan	3,301	29,365	12.3
4	Brazil	2,166	14,393	8.0
5	Switzerland	1,124	9,769	4.2
6	Italy	1,048	5,725	3.9
7	Germany	845	8,899	3.1
8	France	724	6,900	2.7
9	Thailand	646	7,439	2.4
10	China	573	5,892	2.1
11	Turkey	558	5,463	2.1
12	Argentina	420	2,416	1.6
13	Saudi Arabia	386	5,067	1.4
14	Spain	286	2,081	1.1
15	Mexico	233	2,398	0.9
16	Indonesia	204	2,116	0.8
17	Austria	197	1,863	0.7
18	Colombia	190	1,871	0.7
	State Totals	**26,925**	**247,102**	

NEW YORK

Rank	Place of Origin	Students	Student-Weeks	% of Students
1	Korea, Republic of	2,126	30,832	23.1
2	Japan	2,085	28,673	22.6
3	Taiwan	1,087	7,633	11.8
4	Turkey	680	6,545	7.4
5	Brazil	402	3,357	4.4
6	Colombia	301	2,793	3.3
7	China	297	4,181	3.2
8	France	202	1,429	2.2
9	Italy	175	1,418	1.9
10	Germany	138	1,131	1.5
11	Argentina	116	944	1.3
12	Venezuela	102	1,166	1.1
13	Indonesia	99	404	1.1
14	Dominican Republic	87	473	0.9
15	Mexico	82	787	0.9
16	Russia	70	899	0.8
17	Spain	68	563	0.7
18	Poland	65	745	0.7
	State Totals	**9,217**	**104,276**	

TEXAS

Rank	Place of Origin	Students	Student-Weeks	% of Students
1	Mexico	3,297	31,841	55.4
2	Korea, Republic of	544	9,152	9.1
3	Taiwan	366	6,742	6.1
4	Japan	363	5,996	6.1
5	Colombia	252	4,359	4.2
6	Venezuela	184	3,230	3.1
7	Brazil	148	1,565	2.5
8	Turkey	118	1,647	2.0
9	Thailand	115	2,469	1.9
10	China	96	1,472	1.6
11	Saudi Arabia	95	1,514	1.6
12	Argentina	58	631	1.0
13	Peru	48	777	0.8
14	Vietnam	43	809	0.7
15	Morocco	40	635	0.7

FLORIDA

Rank	Place of Origin	Students	Student-Weeks	% of Students
1	Brazil	710	4,554	17.6
2	Venezuela	606	5,300	15.1
3	Japan	411	4,786	10.2
4	Italy	301	1,420	7.5
5	Saudi Arabia	299	3,839	7.4
6	Colombia	251	2,715	6.2
7	Korea, Republic of	205	1,914	5.1
8	France	130	602	3.2
9	Turkey	123	1,247	3.1
10	Argentina	116	884	2.9
11	Spain	92	647	2.3
12	Switzerland	84	612	2.1
13	Germany	52	319	1.3
14	Taiwan	50	641	1.2
15	Mexico	49	365	1.2

37 LEADING 18 PLACES OF ORIGIN FOR IEP STUDENTS IN SELECTED LEADING HOST STATES, 2001

TEXAS (cont'd)					FLORIDA (cont'd)				
Rank	Place of Origin	Students	Student-Weeks	% of Students	Rank	Place of Origin	Students	Student-Weeks	% of Students
16	Lebanon	40	564	0.7	16	Peru	44	538	1.1
17	Russia	27	576	0.5	17	Ecuador	44	394	1.1
18	Spain	26	375	0.4	18	Thailand	38	459	0.9
State Totals		**5,956**	**78,390**		**State Totals**		**4,024**	**35,912**	

37 (cont'd) LEADING 18 PLACES OF ORIGIN FOR IEP STUDENTS IN SELECTED LEADING HOST STATES, 2001

Program Type/Membership	Number of Programs	Total Number of Students	Total Taking Less Than 18 Hours	Total Taking More Than 18 Hours	Total Number of Student-Weeks	Student-Weeks Less Than 18 Hours	Student-Weeks More Than 18 Hours
Independent for-profit affiliated by contract with an institution of higher education	60	30,147	3,939	8,521	279,433	31,894	82,563
Independent for-profit not affiliated by contract with an institution of higher education	16	11,431	1,747	6,848	122,941	10,310	68,571
Independent not-for-profit affiliated by contract with an institution of higher education	2	312	4	307	3,074	32	3,042
Independent not-for-profit not affiliated by contract with an institution of higher education	6	1,989	70	1,793	13,313	358	12,955
Private college or university governed	35	7,667	2,494	4,677	106,820	30,199	58,234
Public college or university governed	77	26,975	2,838	23,810	340,022	36,626	259,803
Membership Affiliation							
AAIEP Only	112	54,481	6,781	26,987	549,415	61,393	266,985
UCIEP Only	13	3,266	675	2,236	50,087	7,610	24,808
Both AAIEP & UCIEP	33	14,777	1,752	12,700	185,799	18,079	155,268
Neither	38	5,997	1,884	4,033	80,301	22,337	38,107
All Programs	**196**	**78,521**	**11,092**	**45,956**	**865,603**	**109,419**	**485,168**

38 IEP STUDENTS AND STUDENT-WEEKS BY PROGRAM TYPE AND AFFILIATION, 2001

INTERNATIONAL SCHOLARS

Place of Origin	2000/01	2001/02	% Change	Place of Origin	2000/01	2001/02	% Change
AFRICA	**2,256**	**2,788**	**23.6**	**West Africa**	**384**	**660**	**71.9**
				Benin	2	10	400.0
East Africa	**406**	**585**	**44.1**	Burkina Faso	5	7	40.0
Burundi	0	7	-	Côte d'Ivoire	21	22	4.8
Comoros	1	0	-100.0	Gambia	6	7	16.7
Eritrea	6	10	66.7	Ghana	75	158	110.7
Ethiopia	52	66	26.9	Guinea	4	6	50.0
Kenya	136	229	68.4	Liberia	4	13	225.0
Madagascar	6	7	16.7	Mali	7	14	100.0
Malawi	10	7	-30.0	Mauritania	7	4	-42.9
Mauritius	12	10	-16.7	Niger	12	18	50.0
Mozambique	6	15	150.0	Nigeria	176	335	90.3
Rwanda	7	0	-100.0	Senegal	45	46	2.2
Somalia	4	7	75.0	Sierra Leone	16	14	-12.5
Tanzania	29	54	86.2	Togo	4	6	50.0
Uganda	38	52	36.8				
Zambia	32	40	25.0	**ASIA**	**35,620**	**39,122**	**9.8**
Zimbabwe	67	81	20.9				
				East Asia	**27,899**	**30,081**	**7.8**
Central Africa	**81**	**121**	**49.4**	China	14,772	15,624	5.8
Angola	1	7	600.0	Hong Kong	150	190	26.7
Cameroon	56	73	30.4	Japan	5,905	5,736	-2.9
Central African Republic	1	4	300.0	Korea, Dem. People's Rep.	17	47	176.5
Chad	7	8	14.3	Korea, Republic of	5,830	7,143	22.5
Congo	10	11	10.0	Macao	2	1	-50.0
Equatorial Guinea	0	7	-	Mongolia	27	46	70.4
Gabon	1	1	0.0	Taiwan	1,196	1,294	8.2
Zaire/Congo	5	10	100.0				
				South & Central Asia	**6,422**	**7,452**	**16.0**
North Africa	**1,015**	**935**	**-7.9**	Afghanistan	6	8	33.3
Algeria	86	75	-12.8	Bangladesh	236	283	19.9
Canary Islands	2	1	-50.0	Bhutan	6	1	-83.3
Egypt	671	622	-7.3	India	5,456	6,249	14.5
Libya	2	1	-50.0	Kazakhstan	53	46	-13.2
Morocco	159	148	-6.9	Kyrgyzstan	28	32	14.3
Sudan	28	28	0.0	Nepal	75	103	37.3
Tunisia	67	60	-10.4	Pakistan	372	470	26.3
				Republic of Maldives	1	0	-100.0
Southern Africa	**370**	**487**	**31.6**	Sri Lanka	131	171	30.5
Botswana	36	32	-11.1	Tajikistan	9	18	100.0
Lesotho	1	3	200.0	Turkmenistan	5	17	240.0
Namibia	1	8	700.0	Uzbekistan	44	54	22.7
South Africa	327	438	33.9				
Swaziland	5	6	20.0	**Southeast Asia**	**1,299**	**1,589**	**22.3**
				Brunei	2	0	-100.0
				Cambodia	5	21	320.0

39 INTERNATIONAL SCHOLAR TOTALS BY PLACE OF ORIGIN, 2000/01 & 2001/02

Place of Origin	2000/01	2001/02	% Change		Place of Origin	2000/01	2001/02	% Change
Indonesia	210	241	14.8		Italy	2,226	2,257	1.4
Laos	2	3	50.0		Liechtenstein	2	0	-100.0
Malaysia	153	218	42.5		Luxembourg	12	11	-8.3
Myanmar	26	20	-23.1		Malta	6	1	-83.3
Philippines	265	297	12.1		Netherlands	1,037	1,001	-3.5
Singapore	162	226	39.5		Norway	359	379	5.6
Thailand	377	449	19.1		Portugal	260	269	3.5
Vietnam	97	114	17.5		San Marino	1	0	-100.0
					Spain	1,706	1,822	6.8
EUROPE	**28,668**	**28,769**	**0.4**		Sweden	711	738	3.8
					Switzerland	767	653	-14.9
Eastern Europe	**7,312**	**7,764**	**6.2**		United Kingdom	3,352	3,314	-1.1
Albania	34	45	32.4					
Armenia	73	73	0.0		**LATIN AMERICA**	**4,676**	**5,988**	**28.1**
Azerbaijan	28	22	-21.4					
Belarus	95	105	10.5		**Caribbean**	**275**	**815**	**196.4**
Bosnia & Herzegovina	33	39	18.2		Antigua	2	3	50.0
Bulgaria	295	314	6.4		Aruba	2	1	-50.0
Croatia	136	153	12.5		Bahamas	11	45	309.1
Czech Republic	315	347	10.2		Barbados	15	33	120.0
Czechoslovakia, Former	6	14	133.3		British Virgin Islands	4	6	50.0
Estonia	41	47	14.6		Cuba	69	43	-37.7
Georgia	123	148	20.3		Dominica	2	3	50.0
Hungary	467	501	7.3		Dominican Republic	27	43	59.3
Latvia	29	39	34.5		Grenada	0	7	-
Lithuania	91	85	-6.6		Guadeloupe	1	0	-100.0
Macedonia	27	42	55.6		Haiti	7	14	100.0
Moldova	38	75	97.4		Jamaica	64	275	329.7
Poland	862	980	13.7		Martinique	1	3	200.0
Romania	440	586	33.2		Montserrat	2	1	-50.0
Russia	3,253	3,123	-4.0		Netherlands Antilles	4	11	175.0
Slovakia	120	141	17.5		St. Kitts-Nevis	4	6	50.0
Slovenia	61	66	8.2		St. Lucia	0	7	-
Ukraine	564	608	7.8		St. Vincent	4	8	100.0
Yugoslavia, Former	181	211	16.6		Trinidad & Tobago	56	303	441.1
					Turks & Caicos Islands	0	3	
Western Europe	**21,356**	**21,005**	**-1.6**					
Austria	439	445	1.4		**Central America/Mexico**	**1,088**	**1,300**	**19.5**
Belgium	354	340	-4.0		Belize	10	14	40.0
Denmark	458	415	-9.4		Costa Rica	71	79	11.3
Finland	337	332	-1.5		El Salvador	13	13	0.0
France	3,154	2,985	-5.4		Guatemala	35	35	0.0
Germany	5,221	5,028	-3.7		Honduras	19	38	100.0
Greece	558	569	2.0		Mexico	898	1,068	18.9
Iceland	36	43	19.4		Nicaragua	15	17	13.3
Ireland	360	403	11.9		Panama	27	36	33.3

39 (cont'd) INTERNATIONAL SCHOLAR TOTALS BY PLACE OF ORIGIN, 2000/01 & 2001/02

Place of Origin	2000/01	2001/02	% Change	Place of Origin	2000/01	2001/02	% Change
South America	**3,313**	**3,873**	**16.9**	Palestinian Authority	15	20	33.3
Argentina	638	837	31.2	Qatar	2	3	50.0
Bolivia	35	50	42.9	Saudi Arabia	83	86	3.6
Brazil	1,315	1,493	13.5	Syria	75	70	-6.7
Chile	243	229	-5.8	Turkey	918	1,141	24.3
Colombia	404	514	27.2	United Arab Emirates	5	8	60.0
Ecuador	64	93	45.3	Yemen	6	6	0.0
Guyana	9	14	55.6				
Paraguay	7	15	114.3	**NORTH AMERICA**	**3,739**	**3,916**	**4.7**
Peru	212	212	0.0	Bermuda	4	11	175.0
Suriname	7	10	42.9	Canada	3,735	3,905	4.6
Uruguay	62	66	6.5				
Venezuela	317	340	7.3	**OCEANIA**	**1,576**	**1,747**	**10.9**
				Australia	1,212	1,316	8.6
MIDDLE EAST	**3,108**	**3,578**	**15.1**	Kiribati	1	1	0.0
Bahrain	2	3	50.0	Fiji	1	1	0.0
Cyprus	52	46	-11.5	New Zealand	359	428	19.2
Iran	387	502	29.7	Papua New Guinea	2	1	-50.0
Iraq	22	31	40.9	Tonga	1	0	-100.0
Israel	1,205	1,270	5.4				
Jordan	131	155	18.3	**STATELESS**	**0**	**110**	**-**
Kuwait	29	24	-17.2				
Lebanon	169	206	21.9	**WORLD TOTAL**	**79,651**	**86,015**	**8.0**
Oman	7	7	0.0				

39 (cont'd) INTERNATIONAL SCHOLAR TOTALS BY PLACE OF ORIGIN, 2000/01 & 2001/02

Rank	Institution	City	State	2000/01	2001/02
1	Harvard University	Cambridge	MA	2,644	2,884
2	University of California – Los Angeles	Los Angeles	CA	1,759	2,496
3	University of California – Berkeley	Berkeley	CA	2,477	2,365
4	Stanford University	Stanford	CA	1,795	1,886
5	University of California – San Diego	La Jolla	CA	1,661	1,878
6	University of Pennsylvania	Philadelphia	PA	1,774	1,774
7	Massachusetts Institute of Technology	Cambridge	MA	1,679	1,640
8	University of Illinois at Urbana–Champaign	Champaign	IL	1,225	1,623
9	Columbia University	New York	NY	1,398	1,621
10	University of California – San Francisco	San Francisco	CA	1,492	1,492
11	University of Washington	Seattle	WA	1,506	1,489
12	Yale University	New Haven	CT	1,228	1,478
13	The Ohio State University Main Campus	Columbus	OH	1,480	1,378
14	Penn State University Park	University Park	PA	749	1,370
15	University of Michigan – Ann Arbor	Ann Arbor	MI	1,342	1,342
16	University of Florida	Gainesville	FL	1,178	1,318
17	University of Minnesota – Twin Cities	Minneapolis	MN	1,271	1,271
18	University of California – Davis	Davis	CA	1,250	1,250
19	University of Wisconsin – Madison	Madison	WI	1,078	1,129
20	University of Southern California	Los Angeles	CA	997	1,112
21	University of Illinois at Chicago	Chicago	IL	1,189	1,106
22	Cornell University	Ithaca	NY	1,039	1,076
23	University of North Carolina at Chapel Hill	Chapel Hill	NC	938	1,017
24	University of California – Irvine	Irvine	CA	1,011	1,011
25	Washington University	St. Louis	MO	999	989
26	University of Texas at Austin	Austin	TX	934	962
27	Boston University	Boston	MA	841	909
28	Texas A & M University	College Station	TX	903	903
29	University of Iowa	Iowa City	IA	901	901
30	Michigan State University	East Lansing	MI	719	880

40 INSTITUTIONS HOSTING THE MOST INTERNATIONAL SCHOLARS, 2000/01 & 2001/02

State	1993/94 Total	1994/95 Total	1995/96 Total	1996/97 Total	1997/98 Total	1998/99 Total	1999/00 Total	2000/01 Total	2001/02 Total	% Change
Alabama	808	652	591	659	765	507	763	898	893	-0.6
Alaska	31	50	24	31	31	0*	0*	0*	0*	-
Arizona	688	515	835	887	889	1,095	1,199	1,191	1,168	-1.9
Arkansas	207	214	307	157	199	138	126	161	175	8.7
California	9,986	10,314	11,723	10,485	11,530	13,311	13,641	13,365	16,236	21.5
Colorado	1,062	1,156	922	946	920	1,109	1,122	1,272	1,376	8.2
Connecticut	60	33	985	1,040	1,100	1,060	1,321	1,360	1,834	34.9
Delaware	793	328	363	366	327	374	677	386	455	17.9
District of Columbia	330	731	779	742	544	741	776	648	610	-5.9
Florida	1,633	1,820	1,661	1,822	1,858	1,770	2,114	2,436	2,552	4.8
Georgia	1,030	1,246	2,201	1,434	1,592	1,809	1,844	1,780	1,852	4.0
Hawaii	975	188	188	234	293	296	296	376	446	18.6
Idaho	54	46	321	272	76	64	103	113	136	20.4
Illinois	2,340	2,374	1,741	2,847	2,892	3,379	3,545	4,048	4,392	8.5
Indiana	1,700	1,438	1,550	1,672	1,754	1,600	1,994	1,826	1,950	6.8
Iowa	830	774	922	1,139	941	1,260	1,276	1,500	1,441	-3.9
Kansas	595	362	313	413	343	423	425	581	451	-22.4
Kentucky	305	368	445	482	517	580	412	600	635	5.8
Louisiana	444	539	505	486	591	567	851	626	713	13.9
Maine	47	63	54	28	34	81	75	116	159	37.1
Maryland	912	668	737	1,117	1,647	1,059	1,417	1,506	1,965	30.5
Massachusetts	5,807	5,185	5,274	5,044	5,219	5,184	5,181	6,180	6,340	2.6
Michigan	1,402	2,165	1,725	2,430	2,253	2,356	2,694	2,930	3,137	7.1
Minnesota	1,306	1,227	1,231	1,197	1,255	1,281	1,260	1,271	1,475	16.1
Mississippi	255	178	171	164	161	232	302	285	347	21.8
Missouri	2,154	1,473	1,429	1,485	1,509	1,387	1,454	1,681	1,706	1.5
Montana	73	93	113	128	112	132	133	248	234	-5.6
Nebraska	281	300	244	357	207	538	312	537	599	11.5
Nevada	141	98	185	167	173	285	185	199	257	29.1
New Hampshire	188	195	240	234	324	355	443	468	437	-6.6
New Jersey	1,006	919	520	472	558	630	564	1,209	1,195	-1.2
New Mexico	200	210	222	168	257	239	237	304	340	11.8
New York	4,620	4,599	4,067	4,311	4,468	5,262	5,309	5,728	5,847	2.1
North Carolina	1,511	1,424	1,463	1,414	1,776	1,684	1,968	2,145	2,581	20.3
North Dakota	174	53	57	98	87	85	91	139	129	-7.2
Ohio	1,681	1,862	1,920	2,103	2,525	2,500	2,646	2,559	2,330	-8.9
Oklahoma	363	450	219	456	432	659	548	472	388	-17.8
Oregon	878	715	792	729	756	762	763	794	837	5.4

41 INTERNATIONAL SCHOLARS BY STATE, 1993/94 – 2001/02

1993/94 State	1994/95 Total	1995/96 Total	1996/97 Total	1997/98 Total	1998/99 Total	1999/00 Total	2000/01 Total	2001/02 Total	% Total	Change
Pennsylvania	3,594	3,681	3,277	4,012	3,858	4,357	4,557	4,655	5,463	17.4
Rhode Island	281	341	399	449	434	408	383	528	528	0.0
South Carolina	486	469	422	547	964	913	1,021	810	746	-7.9
South Dakota	19	10	23	35	14	21	8	18	17	-5.6
Tennessee	1,105	1,197	1,000	1,087	893	1,055	1,169	1,751	1,663	-5.0
Texas	3,610	3,574	3,243	3,616	3,636	4,288	4,686	4,349	4,885	12.3
Utah	338	448	383	505	511	558	567	669	492	-26.5
Vermont	228	207	200	189	209	203	228	231	0*	-
Virginia	1,030	1,015	1,017	1,042	1,191	1,427	1,423	1,553	1,438	-7.4
Washington	1,202	1,215	1,309	1,397	1,465	1,585	1,659	1,809	1,786	-1.3
West Virginia	53	54	40	28	33	32	33	44	38	-13.6
Wisconsin	1,044	750	888	1,077	1,243	730	652	1,191	1,247	4.7
Wyoming	65	56	103	83	83	85	85	71	66	-7.0
Puerto Rico	56	32	60	71	45	45	33	34	28	-17.6
U.S. TOTAL	**59,981**	**58,074**	**59,403**	**62,354**	**65,494**	**70,501**	**74,571**	**79,651**	**86,015**	**8.0**

* Data not provided

41   (cont d) INTERNATIONAL SCHOLARS BY STATE, 1993/94 — 2001/02

Characteristic	1993/94	1994/95	1995/96	1996/97	1997/98	1998/99	1999/00	2000/01	2001/02
				PERCENT OF INTERNATIONAL SCHOLARS					
Visa Status									
J (All)	73.8	76.6	77.0	75.9	73.2	74.3	.	.	.
J-1	.	.	.	.	.	.	69.0	68.5	64.0
J-1 Other	.	.	.	.	.	.	2.6	2.3	2.7
H-1B	17.8	16.0	16.2	17.6	18.3	18.8	20.5	22.0	24.6
TN	.	.	.	.	.	.	1.5	1.6	1.6
O-1	.	.	.	.	.	.	0.8	1.1	1.2
Other	8.4	7.4	6.8	6.5	8.5	6.8	5.5	4.4	5.9
Sex									
Male	75.0	73.8	73.7	74.2	73.7	72.0	71.8	70.5	69.3
Female	25.0	26.2	26.3	25.8	26.3	28.0	28.2	29.5	30.7
Primary Function									
Research	79.8	80.7	82.6	81.9	83.1	81.0	76.5	79.2	77.2
Teaching	12.1	12.2	11.5	11.5	11.5	10.9	10.4	10.8	11.7

42   VISA STATUS, SEX, AND PRIMARY FUNCTION OF INTERNATIONAL SCHOLARS IN THE UNITED STATES, 1993/94 — 2001/02

Characteristic	1993/94	1994/95	1995/96	1996/97	1997/98	1998/99	1999/00	2000/01	2001/02
PERCENT OF INTERNATIONAL SCHOLARS									
Both Res. & Teach.	8.1	7.1	5.9	6.6	5.4	8.1	7.8	5.0	4.9
Other	.	.	.	.	.	.	5.3	5.0	6.2
TOTAL	**59,981**	**58,074**	**59,403**	**62,354**	**65,494**	**70,501**	**74,571**	**79,651**	**86,015**

42 (cont'd) VISA STATUS, SEX, AND PRIMARY FUNCTION OF INTERNATIONAL SCHOLARS IN THE UNITED STATES, 1993/94 – 2001/02

Major Field of Specialization	1993/94	1994/95	1995/96	1996/97	1997/98	1998/99	1999/00	2000/01	2001/02
PERCENT OF INTERNATIONAL SCHOLARS									
Health Sciences	27.4	28.6	27.6	27.1	26.9	26.2	23.8	26.9	27.4
Life & Biological Sciences	13.1	14.1	12.8	15.4	14.4	15.4	16.8	14.7	14.6
Physical Sciences	14.7	12.8	14.3	13.8	14.5	15.0	14.8	14.7	14.0
Engineering	11.6	11.9	13.4	11.8	11.7	12.6	11.9	12.6	11.4
Social Sciences & History	4.6	4.0	4.2	4.6	4.6	4.3	3.9	3.6	4.5
Agriculture	3.7	3.4	3.5	4.1	4.0	3.4	3.6	3.9	3.4
Computer & Information Sciences	2.3	2.3	2.7	2.2	2.9	2.5	2.9	2.7	3.3
Business & Management	3.2	2.8	2.9	2.6	2.5	2.3	2.4	2.5	3.1
Mathematics	2.9	2.5	2.8	2.8	2.9	2.8	2.6	2.5	2.6
Other	2.2	3.1	1.5	1.6	2.2	1.5	3.3	2.8	2.4
Foreign Languages & Literature	2.2	2.3	2.0	2.3	1.9	2.3	2.8	1.9	2.0
Education	1.5	1.8	1.6	1.4	1.4	1.4	1.4	1.5	1.5
Area & Ethnic Studies	1.7	1.8	1.5	1.6	1.7	1.8	1.8	1.8	1.4
Letters	1.5	1.4	1.7	1.8	1.6	1.5	1.4	1.3	1.4
Visual & Performing Arts	1.6	1.2	1.7	1.5	1.5	1.4	1.3	1.2	1.3
Law and Legal Studies	1.2	1.1	1.0	1.0	1.0	1.1	1.1	1.2	1.0
Psychology	0.9	0.9	0.9	0.8	1.0	1.0	1.1	1.0	1.0
Philosophy & Religion	1.1	1.1	0.7	0.9	0.7	0.7	0.7	0.6	0.9
Architecture & Environmental Design	0.7	0.7	0.8	0.7	0.6	0.8	0.8	0.7	0.8
Public Affairs	0.7	0.6	0.8	0.7	0.5	0.5	0.5	0.6	0.6
Communications	0.6	0.6	0.6	0.4	0.5	0.5	0.5	0.5	0.6
Home Economics	0.4	0.4	0.4	0.5	0.6	0.6	0.3	0.4	0.5
Library Sciences	0.3	0.2	0.2	0.3	0.3	0.3	0.3	0.3	0.3
Marketing	0.1	0.1	0.1	0.1	0.1	0.1	0.1	0.1	0.1
TOTAL	**59,981**	**58,074**	**59,403**	**62,354**	**65,494**	**70,501**	**74,571**	**79,651**	**86,015**

43 MAJOR FIELD OF SPECIALIZATION OF INTERNATIONAL SCHOLARS, 1993/94 – 2001/02

METHODOLOGY

History of the Census

Since its founding in 1919, the Institute of International Education (IIE) has conducted an annual census of international students in the United States. For the first 30 years, IIE and the Committee on Friendly Relations Among Foreign Students carried out this effort jointly. IIE's first independent publication of the results of the annual census was *Education for One World*, containing data for the 1948/1949 academic year. It was renamed *Open Doors Report on International Educational Exchange* in 1954/1955, and began receiving USIA support (now Department of State) in the early 1970s. *Open Doors* is generally considered the primary source for basic statistics about international students, international scholars, and international students in Intensive English Programs in the United States. The response to this year's *Open Doors* survey (88.4% in 2001/2002) means that the survey constitutes the most comprehensive set of data on the U.S. international student population. IIE also collects baseline data on the participation of U.S. students in for-credit study abroad activity. The Study Abroad Survey is the only national source of information about the involvement of U.S. college students in for-credit study abroad programs.

1000	AFRICA
1100	Eastern Africa
1115	Burundi
1120	Comoros
1105	Djibouti
1195	Eritrea
1125	Ethiopia
1130	Kenya
1135	Madagascar
1140	Malawi
1145	Mauritius
1150	Mozambique
1155	Reunion
1165	Rwanda
1170	Seychelles
1175	Somalia
1180	Tanzania
1185	Uganda
1190	Zambia
1160	Zimbabwe
1200	Central Africa
1210	Angola
1220	Cameroon
1230	Central African Republic
1240	Chad
1250	Congo
1260	Equatorial Guinea
1270	Gabon
1280	São Tomé & Príncipe
1290	Zaire
1300	North Africa
1310	Algeria
1320	Canary Islands
1330	Egypt
1340	Libya
1350	Morocco
1370	Sudan
1380	Tunisia
1360	Western Sahara
1400	Southern Africa
1410	Botswana
1420	Lesotho
1430	Namibia
1440	South Africa
1450	Swaziland
1500	Western Africa
1510	Benin
1585	Burkina Faso

1505	Cape Verde
1535	Côte d'Ivoire
1515	Gambia
1520	Ghana
1525	Guinea
1530	Guinea-Bissau
1540	Liberia
1545	Mali
1550	Mauritania
1555	Niger
1560	Nigeria
1565	St. Helena
1570	Senegal
1575	Sierra Leone
1580	Togo
2000	ASIA
2100	East Asia
2110	China
2120	Taiwan
2130	Hong Kong
2140	Japan
2150	Korea, Democratic People's Republic of
2160	Korea, Republic of
2170	Macao
2180	Mongolia
2200	South & Central Asia
2205	Afghanistan
2210	Bangladesh
2215	Bhutan
2220	India
2260	Kazakhstan
2265	Kyrgyzstan
2225	Maldives, Republic of
2230	Nepal
2235	Pakistan
2245	Sri Lanka
2270	Tajikistan
2250	Turkmenistan
2255	Uzbekistan
2300	Southeast Asia
2305	Brunei
2320	Cambodia
2315	Indonesia
2325	Laos
2330	Malaysia
2310	Myanmar

44 COUNTRY CODES BY COUNTRY WITHIN WORLD REGION

2335	Philippines	3263	Monaco	
2345	Singapore	3266	Netherlands	
2350	Thailand	3270	Norway	
2360	Vietnam	3273	Portugal	
2370	East Timor	3276	San Marino	
		3280	Spain	
3000	EUROPE	3283	Sweden	
3100	Eastern Europe	3286	Switzerland	
3110	Albania	3290	United Kingdom	
3189	Armenia	3240	Vatican City	
3174	Azerbaijan			
3181	Belarus	4000	LATIN AMERICA	
3193	Bosnia & Herzegovina	4100	Caribbean	
3120	Bulgaria	4103	Aruba	
3191	Croatia	4105	Bahamas	
3131	Czech Republic	4110	Barbados	
3130	Czechoslovakia, Former	4115	Cayman Islands	
3183	Estonia	4120	Cuba	
3188	Georgia	4125	Dominican Republic	
3150	Hungary	4130	Guadeloupe	
3184	Latvia	4135	Haiti	
3185	Lithuania	4140	Jamaica	
3194	Macedonia	4150	Leeward Islands	
3187	Moldova	4155	Anguilla	
3160	Poland	4151	Antigua	
3170	Romania	4152	British Virgin Islands	
3186	Russia	4153	Montserrat	
3132	Slovakia	4154	St. Kitts-Nevis	
3192	Slovenia	4160	Martinique	
3182	Ukraine	4170	Netherlands Antilles	
3180	U.S.S.R., Former	4180	Trinidad & Tobago	
3190	Yugoslavia, Former	4185	Turks & Caicos Isles	
3200	Western Europe	4190	Windward Islands	
3203	Andorra	4191	Dominica	
3206	Austria	4192	Grenada	
3210	Belgium	4193	St. Lucia	
3213	Denmark	4194	St. Vincent	
3220	Finland	4200	Central America/Mexico	
3223	France	4210	Belize	
3226	Germany	4230	Costa Rica	
3233	Gibraltar	4240	El Salvador	
3236	Greece	4250	Guatemala	
3243	Iceland	4260	Honduras	
3246	Ireland	4270	Mexico	
3250	Italy	4280	Nicaragua	
3253	Liechtenstein	4290	Panama	
3256	Luxembourg	4300	South America	
3260	Malta			

44 (cont'd) COUNTRY CODES BY COUNTRY WITHIN WORLD REGION

Imputation

Throughout this document, student counts other than the total international student enrollments, U.S. study abroad totals, scholar totals, and IEP totals are determined by imputation. Estimates of the number of students for each of the variables collected by the various surveys are imputed from the total number of students reported. For each imputation, base or raw counts are multiplied by a correction factor that reflects the ratio of difference between the sum of the categories being imputed and the total number of students reported by institutions. It should be noted that student numbers vary slightly within this publication. Due to rounding, percentages do not always add up to 100%. This is also true for some imputations. In these instances the total percent column is listed as 100% to indicate that all categories are accounted for. The data collection methodology was designed to produce stable, national estimates of international education activity. Analysis for units that reflect relatively small numbers of students (certain nationalities, fields of study, sources of financial support) and especially those that are cut by other variables may reflect greater error variation than variables with a larger response base. A relatively large discrepancy exists between the academic level figures reported by country and those provided for all foreign students in general. This discrepancy results from the differential response rates to the nationality question and the academic level question.

Country Classification System

The classification of countries into regional groupings that is used throughout this report follows IIE practices that were originated when the *Open Doors* Census was first conducted in 1948. (Table 44)

4305	Argentina
4310	Bolivia
4315	Brazil
4320	Chile
4325	Colombia
4330	Ecuador
4335	Falkland Islands
4340	French Guiana
4345	Guyana
4350	Paraguay
4355	Peru
4360	Suriname
4365	Uruguay
4370	Venezuela
2400	**MIDDLE EAST**
2405	Bahrain
2410	Cyprus
2415	Iran
2420	Iraq
2425	Israel
2430	Jordan
2435	Kuwait
2440	Lebanon
2445	Oman
2443	Palestinian Authority
2450	Qatar
2455	Saudi Arabia
2460	Syria
2465	Turkey
2470	United Arab Emirates
2485	Yemen

5000	**NORTH AMERICA**
5110	Bermuda
5120	Canada
6000	**OCEANIA**
6100	**Australia & New Zealand**
6110	Australia
6120	New Zealand
6200	**Pacific Ocean Island Areas**
6210	Cook Islands
6215	Fiji
6220	French Polynesia
6225	Kiribati
6227	Marshall Islands
6260	Micronesia, Federated States of
6230	Nauru
6235	New Caledonia
6250	Niue
6255	Norfolk Island
6263	Palau
6240	Papua New Guinea
6205	Solomon Islands
6270	Tonga
6271	Tuvalu
6245	Vanuatu
6275	Wallis & Futuna Isles
6280	Western Samoa

44 (cont'd) COUNTRY CODES BY COUNTRY WITHIN WORLD REGION

AGRICULTURE
01 Agricultural Business and Production
02 Agricultural Sciences
03 Conservation and Renewable Natural Resources

ARCHITECTURE AND RELATED PROGRAMS
04 Architecture and Related Programs

AREA, ETHNIC, AND CULTURAL STUDIES
05 Area, Ethnic, and Cultural Studies

BUSINESS MANAGEMENT AND ADMINISTRATIVE SERVICES
52 Business Management and Administrative Services
08 Marketing Operations and Distribution

COMMUNICATIONS
09 Communications
10 Communication Technologies

COMPUTER AND INFORMATION SCIENCES
11 Computer and Information Sciences

PERSONAL AND MISCELLANEOUS SERVICES
12 Personal and Miscellaneous Services

EDUCATION
13 Education

ENGINEERING
14 Engineering
15 Engineering-Related Technologies

FOREIGN LANGUAGES AND LITERATURE
16 Foreign Languages and Literature

HEALTH
51 Health Professions and Related Sciences

HOME ECONOMICS
19 Home Economics
20 Vocational Home Economics

LAW AND LEGAL STUDIES
22 Law and Legal Studies

ENGLISH LANGUAGE AND LITERATURE/LETTERS
23 English Language and Literature/Letters

LIBERAL/GENERAL STUDIES
24 Liberal/General Studies

45   FIELD OF STUDY CATEGORY CODES

Fields of Study and U.S. Regions

The fields of study used in this book are those from *Classification of Instructional Programs, 1990*, published by the National Center for Education Statistics (NCES) of the U.S. Department of Education. The updated 2000 edition was used in the data editing for this year's *Open Doors*. See Table 45 for a list of major fields of study.

About the Annual Census of International Students

The Higher Education Resource Group of IIE obtained the data presented in *Open Doors 2002* through a survey conducted, in Fall 2001 thru Spring 2002, of campus officials in 2,697 regionally accredited institutions of higher education in the United States. Of the institutions surveyed, 2,384 or 88.4% responded to the questionnaire, as is shown in Table 46. The response rate, although always high, has fluctuated over the history of the Census, reaching the lowest point in the mid-1970s. However, in the past decade it has been very high, ranging from 92.6% in 1979/1980 to 99.5% in 1987/1988, then dipping to 88.4% this year. This slip in response rate brings the overall response to the Census to the lowest point seen in more than 10 years. The relatively sharp fall off in response rate noted this year might reflect the cumulative effect of the demands on campus-based data providers from changes in reporting requirements coming from federal sources, including the IPEDS survey and the rollout of the new SEVIS data collection system.

Over nine-tenths (2,284) of the institutions that responded to the survey reported enrolling international students (Table 46). Of the schools with international students, a total of 422 (representing 17.7%) provided only total international student counts (Step 1), as shown in Table 47. The majority (82.3%), however, provided information not only on the total but also on the students' country of origin, field of study, academic level, sex, and other characteristics (Step 2) as well.

LIBRARY SCIENCES
25   Library Sciences

LIFE SCIENCES
26   Biological Sciences/Life Sciences

MATHEMATICS
27   Mathematics

MILITARY TECHNOLOGIES
29   Military Technologies

MULTI/INTERDISCIPLINARY STUDIES
30   Multi/Interdisciplinary Studies

PARKS, RECREATION, LEISURE, AND FITNESS STUDIES
31   Parks, Recreation, and Leisure Studies

PHILOSOPHY AND RELIGION
38   Philosophy
39   Theological Studies and Religious Vocations

PHYSICAL SCIENCES
40   Physical Sciences
41   Science Technologies

PSYCHOLOGY
42   Psychology

PROTECTIVE SERVICES AND PUBLIC ADMINISTRATION
43   Protective Services
44   Public Administration and Services

SOCIAL SCIENCES AND HISTORY
45   Social Sciences

TRADE AND INDUSTRIAL
46   Construction Trades
47   Mechanics and Repairs
48   Precision Production
49   Transportation and Material Moving

VISUAL AND PERFORMING ARTS
50   Visual and Performing Arts

INTENSIVE ENGLISH LANGUAGE
60   Intensive English Language

UNDECLARED
90   Undeclared

* Source: National Center for Educational Statistics, *Classification of Instructional Programs, 1990* (Washington, D.C.: NCES, 1991).

45   (cont'd) FIELD OF STUDY CATEGORY CODES

Year	Institutions Surveyed	Institutions w/ Int'l Students	Institutions w/o Int'l Students	Total Responding Institutions	% Response
1964/65	2,556	1,859	434	2,293	89.7
1969/70	2,859	1,734	265	1,999	69.9
1974/75	3,085	1,760	148	1,908	61.8
1979/80	3,186	2,651	299	2,950	92.6
1984/85	2,833	2,492	274	2,766	97.6
1989/90	2,891	2,546	294	2,840	98.2
1990/91	2,879	2,543	241	2,784	96.7
1991/92	2,823	2,436	228	2,646	94.4
1992/93	2,783	2,417	166	2,583	92.8
1993/94	2,743	2,451	163	2,614	95.3
1994/95	2,758	2,517	167	2,684	97.3
1995/96	2,715	2,403	176	2,579	95.7
1996/97	2,732	2,428	185	2,613	95.6
1997/98	2,726	2,394	177	2,571	94.3
1998/99	2,708	2,446	142	2,588	95.6
1999/00	2,696	2,367	126	2,493	92.5
2000/01	2,699	2,344	120	2,464	91.3
2001/02	2,697	2,284	100	2,384	88.4

46 INSTITUTIONS SURVEYED AND TYPE OF RESPONSE, SELECTED YEARS 1964/65 – 2001/02

Type of Response	1999/00 Number	%	2000/01 Number	%	2001/02 Number	%
Total Only - STEP 1	768	30.8	509	20.7	422	17.7
Institutional Data - STEP 2	1725	69.2	1,955	79.3	1,962	82.3
Total with Students	**2,493**		**2,464**		**2,384**	

47 INSTITUTIONS REPORTING INTERNATIONAL STUDENTS AND TYPE OF RESPONSE, 1999/00 – 2001/02

A high proportion of the colleges and universities with international students sent data on some or all of the characteristics on the questionnaire, as Table 48 shows. Some variables commanded a greater number of responses: data on country of origin exist for 84.9% of all international students reported, and field of study breakdowns for 82.9%. Conversely, information on the students' primary source of funding and on their marital status is available for less than half of the total number reported (40.0% and 38.3%, respectively).

About the International Scholar Survey

For the purposes of this survey, international scholars are defined as non-immigrant, non-student academics (teachers and/or researchers, administrators). Other scholars may be affiliated with U.S. institutions for other activities such as conferences, colloquia, observations, consultations, or other short-term professional development activities. The survey was limited to doctoral degree-granting institutions where most J Visa scholars are based. This year was the third year that the survey was conducted through the web and a more detailed breakout of visa categories was sought. The institutions polled were asked to give us as much information as possible on scholars who were at their institutions for part or all of the period beginning on July 1, 2001 and ending June 30, 2002. The forms requested information on the primary function of the scholars (research, teaching, both, or other), on their geographic origin, field of specialization, sex, and immigration status. Responses were received from 264 of the 348 institutions polled, a response rate of 75.9%, which is sharply off from the 81.0% obtained last year. This drop is consistent with that seen for the international student census. Not all institutions reporting international scholars in 2001/2002 were able to provide detailed information on the characteristics of their scholars. The proportion of institutions that were able to give breakdowns for individual variables ranged from 76.7% for visa status to 67.3% for field of specialization. The general drop in response rates to individual variables over the previous year seen in Table 49 may be part of the general difficulty the project has had with data collection this year.

About the U.S. Study Abroad Survey

This survey focuses on study abroad for academic credit. The study abroad population has been narrowly defined as only those students who received academic credit from a U.S. accredited institution of higher education after they returned from their study abroad experience. Students studying abroad without credit transfers are not included here nor are U.S. students enrolled overseas for degrees. The number of students who receive academic credit is inevitably lower than the number of all students who go abroad. Hence, the figures presented here give a conservative picture of study abroad activity. Study abroad information was obtained from 1,072 or 84.3% of the 1,272 surveyed institutions.

Category	Base Number	% of Int'l Students
Academic Level	513,626	88.1
Country of Origin	494,868	84.9
Field of Study	483,076	82.9
Sex	477,703	81.9
Visa (Immigration) Status	472,325	81.0
Enrollment Status	458,398	78.6
Primary Source of Funds	233,414	40.0
Marital Status	223,090	38.3
Total Reported	**582,996**	

48 INSTITUTIONS REPORTING INTERNATIONAL STUDENTS BY INDIVIDUAL VARIABLES, 2001/02

	1994/95 %	1995/96 %	1996/97 %	1997/98 %	1998/99 %	1999/00 %	2000/01 %	2001/02 %
Visa Status	92.4	90.8	92.9	84.2	94.8	70.4	85.5	76.7
Country of Origin	86.6	88.3	90.8	83.6	88.9	94.5	82.3	71.7
Sex	83.2	81.3	88.3	80.2	82.9	64.8	79.4	70.8
Primary Function	75.2	77.1	88.2	69.2	81.9	67.7	76.9	70.3
Field of Specialization	90.5	85.9	88.4	84.0	87.8	65.9	78.9	67.3
Total	**58,074**	**59,403**	**62,354**	**65,494**	**70,501**	**74,571**	**79,651**	**86,015**

49 RESPONSE RATE TO INDIVIDUAL VARIABLES: INTERNATIONAL SCHOLAR SURVEY, 1994/95 – 2001/02

Not all institutions that reported giving credit for study abroad in 2000/2001 provided detailed information about the characteristics of the students, as shown in Table 50. The proportion of schools that gave breakdowns for individual variables ranged from 50.3% for race/ethnicity to 92.1% for program duration. The survey included an item on internships and work abroad for the third year.

About the Intensive English Program Survey

In 1999, IIE and two leading professional intensive English associations, AAIEP and UCIEP, joined to inaugurate an initiative to collect national data that reflects IEP activity in the U.S. Now in its third year, this effort to collect data with the sponsorship and support of the professional associations reflects the growth of independent and affiliated proprietary programs. Data elements included program sponsor-

Category	1991/92 %	1993/94 %	1994/95 %	1995/96 %	1996/97 %	1997/98 %	1998/99 %	1999/00 %	2000/01 %
Duration of Study	79.4	93.1	77.7	91.2	89.8	85.9	89.5	92.5	92.1
Host Country	83.6	91.3	79.5	91.0	88.4	80.6	86.3	92.2	91.4
Program Sponsorship	-	90.7	73.8	92.2	88.7	86.2	87.2	91.0	89.6
Academic Level	65.0	80.1	63.6	77.8	78.5	78.1	79.2	82.1	83.1
Field of Study	46.2	64.3	45.9	60.2	62.8	65.1	65.6	75.1	80.5
Sex	62.6	80.3	65.6	76.1	75.1	75.9	76.3	81.0	80.3
Race/Ethnicity	-	43.3	33.0	39.7	40.9	42.6	44.8	45.7	50.3
Students Reported	**71,154**	**76,302**	**84,403**	**89,242**	**99,448**	**113,959**	**129,770**	**143,590**	**154,168**

50   RESPONSE RATE TO INDIVIDUAL VARIABLES: STUDY ABROAD SURVEY, SELECTED YEARS 1991/92 – 2000/01

Category	Number of Reporting Programs	% of All Participating Programs
Total Number of Students	196	100.0
Program Type	196	100.0
Total Number of Student-Weeks	192	98.0
Duration of Study, Number of Students	156	79.6
Duration of Study, Number of Student-Weeks	143	73.0

Category	Number of Students	% of All Students
Number of Students by Country	77,221	98.3
Number of Student-Weeks by Country	852,372	98.5

51   RESPONSE RATE TO INDIVIDUAL VARIABLES: INTENSIVE ENGLISH PROGRAM SURVEY, 2001

ship, the percentage of students intending to continue further (non-IEP) study in the U.S., program duration (18 hours or more, 18 hours or less), and place of origin. Student totals reflect both headcount enrollment and enrollment by "student-weeks." One student-week equals one student studying for one week. This year, as last year, the number of institutions invited to participate was broadened to include non-AAIEP and UCIEP institutions. These Intensive English Programs were taken from IIE's *Intensive English USA (IEUSA) 2000* directory. In all, 467 programs were contacted by e-mail (257 AAIEP & UCIEP programs and 210 non-members) and returns were obtained from 196 programs for an overall response rate of 42.0%. Responses were obtained from 148 AAIEP & UCIEP institutions, a return of 61.5%, which is up from the 57.6% response last year and comparable to the 61.5% obtained from this group two years ago. Returns were obtained from just 38 non-member programs, for an 18.1% response rate for this group. The 78,521 students reported this year reflects student enrollments throughout the 2001 calendar year (January 1, 2001 to December 31, 2001). The mix of reporting institutions reflects university and college-affiliated programs as well as large for-profit entities that offer English language training. As with our other surveys, not all programs providing total numbers could provide detailed breakouts of place of origin (98.3% of students), duration of study in student-weeks (98.5% of programs), and the percent of students pursuing further study (79.6% of programs). (Table 51)

ACKNOWLEDGEMENTS

Producing the *Open Doors Report* is an intensive year-round project that involves the contributions of many individuals and organizations. The Bureau of Education and Cultural Affairs of the U.S. Department of State has provided the Institute grant support since the 1970s. The grant enables the Institute to collect, analyze, and publish data on international students, U.S. students abroad, and international scholars in the *Open Doors* publication and the *Open Doors* website. Without their generous support, it would be impossible to sustain this extensive research and dissemination effort. The American Association of Intensive English Programs (AAIEP) and University and College Intensive English Programs in the USA (UCIEP), two leading Intensive English Language Program organizations, have provided the Institute support for the Intensive English Program Survey for the past three years.

NAFSA: Association of International Educators and AACRAO, the American Association of Collegiate Registrars and Admissions Officers support the project and provide overall direction for *Open Doors* in its advisory capacity by acting as a sounding board for the field. Kathleen Sideli, Chair of the SECUSSA Data Collection Working Group, spearheaded the initiative and has forged on in her efforts to constantly improve data on study abroad for the study abroad profession and for the field of international education. Lynn Schoch and Jason Baumgartner of Indiana University at Bloomington have assisted us once again with their important analysis of the economic impact of international students on the U.S.

Without the contributions of colleagues at institutions that have responded to the surveys, and especially those who do so year after year, the *Open Doors Report* would not be the comprehensive, reliable data source that it is. Throughout the project, I have called upon many international education professionals and other campus officials in order to put the data into perspective and into the context of international educational activity on campuses. They have graciously taken time out of their busy days to share their insights, thoughts, and "on the ground" experiences with me.

Many individuals outside of the Institute assisted our large staff of two in the production process. The data editors, Leslie Koo, Robin Koo, and Deborah Twiss-McCann edited each and every survey form, question, and data item with great care in order to ensure the integrity of the data. Without their work, we would not be assured of having a solid data set. Marilyn Finkel, Lenora Komlacevs and staff at Automated Data Solutions carefully conducted and monitored the data entry. Renée Meyer's eye for design results in the beautiful layout and cover art of the report. Lori Gilbert, Alan Flint, and staff at Automated Graphic Systems have assisted us through the printing process.

The Institute's leadership, in particular Peggy Blumenthal, Vice-President for Educational Services, provides invaluable support and direction each year for the *Open Doors* project. A special thanks goes to Dr. Todd Davis, who analyzed the data in this publication. He has provided historical perspective to the project and much welcome guidance, oversight, and humor. Daniel Obst, the *IIENetwork* Membership Manager, enables the Institute's members, as well as the public, to have quick and easy access to the data online through his expertise in web management. Debbie Gardner, Heidi Reinholdt and team at Halstead Communications, our public relations firm and Sharon Witherell of the Institute's Office of Public Affairs were instrumental in disseminating the findings of *Open Doors* to the media, and thus, to those outside the field of international education. *Open Doors* is a resource not only for those of us in the field, but for the general public, from students to the press to multinational corporations to government. There has been more interest and awareness about international education from those outside the field since September 11. As we worked on *Open Doors* in the year since that tragic day, we were encouraged by the confirmation that international education continues to be as important as ever and that individuals around the world were not deterred by those terrible events in their pursuit of an international education.

Hey-Kyung Koh Chin
Editor, Open Doors
Program Officer, Higher Education Resource Group
Institute of International Education

New York City
December 2002